Love, Dating ...
And Other Insanities

Relationships Without Regret

Clayton King and Steven Furtick

Published by CJ King Designs

ISBN: 0-9721581-1-1

Love, Dating And Other Insanities
Designed and Published by CJ King Designs
P.O. Box 1448 Boiling Springs, NC 28017

Printed by Hignell Book Printing
488 Burnell Street/Winnipeg, Manitoba, Canada R3G 2B4

From Clayton King

Great big thank you's are deserved by so many. Don't get your feelings hurt if you look for your name here and don't see it, chances are I just forgot to mention you. Primary kudos to Charina Jane Harper King for being the full embodiment of 12 years of desperate prayers from a single young man for a wife. You are everything I need, want, desire, and love. And you will never be able to get rid of me, I am utterly spoiled on you.

Joe and Jane King, my mama and daddy, are simply the best. Everything I am, all that I believe, comes from them. They taught me the blessing of hard work, a love for the church, how to give to God and others, and how to remain faithful to marriage in the most difficult and unimaginable of trials, both physical and emotional. You will never know how much I love you.

For faithful friends, I am grateful. A few names come to mind...Wink, Perry Noble, Ronnie Powell, Mark Baldwin, Chuck Bridges, Mac Powell, Seth Stevens, Matt Orth, Kortland Fuqua, Samuel Thomas, M.A. Thomas, Eddie Mauldin, Brian Burgess, J.D. Greear, Bruce Ashford, Carl Cartee, Grant Campbell, Austin Campbell, Chuck Thompson, Jonathan Martin, Mark Holloway, Ken Mayfield, Joe Teague, Todd Moss, Todd Still, and of course the True Bishop himself, Steven Furtick.

For authors that have ruined me with their books, I am grateful. Mark Twain, Frederick Buechner, C.S. Lewis, Watchman Nee, Dietrich Bonhoeffer, J.R.R.Tolkien, John R.W. Stott, Francis Schaeffer, John Piper, Ravi Zacharias, and John Krakauer. There will be books in Heaven, I am sure, and all the time of eternity to read them all.

For sages and poets with guitars and songs, I am grateful. Mike Roe, Terry Taylor, Derri Daugherty, Gene Eugene, Mike Knott, Bono, Doug Pinnick, Johnny Cash, Bill Malonee, Larry Norman, and Mac Powell.

For the people who have listened to me preach the gospel for years, I am thankful. Clemson, University of Florida, NC State, North Greenville, Anderson College, Newspring, Ebenezer, New Life, Apex, and every church and college that has given me a platform and a microphone. Many thanks. That is all for now.

From Steven Furtick

How could I write on relationships and not thank my wife? Holly, thanks for all you've taught me about washing sheets, matching my clothes, living a deeply honest life and trusting God. Marriage is here (smile)...couldn't be better.

Faith and L-Train, thanks for raising me right. I couldn't have asked for a more loving home to grow up in. Even when it wasn't perfect, it was loving. I love you.

Boitnott family, you're a lot of fun and you gave me a great wife. It's like a sport talking over each other at the dinner table, I'm glad to be a part of your godly family.

It's been fun to write this book with Clayton King, my friend and partner in the gospel. A big thanks to you, Bishop, for being a steady factor in my growth and a real friend who believes in me. I'm glad we did this. "Hey, I've got a title...Love—Waits. Think about that." Thanks to Charie for excellent design work and for putting up with Clayton full time. Verily a crown awaits you.

Thanks to the family of believers and leadership team (too numerous to name) at Christ Covenant Church for helping me learn and grow. You're good people, and the freedom you give me to minister is remarkable.

Thanks to the Crossroads community (all of ya's) for providing structure to my calling. A very special thanks to Kortland Fuqua. You make me aware of the next level and keep us uncomfortable with mediocrity. That's a good thing.

Jerry, thanks for taking time to proof this book.

To Corban Properties Inc. and Corbett Head, Carlos Cortez and the Rock Rangers assisted by Heather M-Kay: Holly and I love you and believe the best is forthcoming.

Thanks to all the youth and college ministries who have hosted me and allowed me to develop this material on the road. It's an honor to labor with you.

Thank You, Jesus, for giving me the gift of purity. Thank You for providing the grace that washes me clean.

The Contents

Chapter 1

The Overview

There is one issue that stands alone as the most thought about, most talked about, most confusing, most all-consuming issue in the life of the average American student. This issue can cause a young man or woman to feel elated, depressed, angry, bewildered, secure, empty and fulfilled-all at the same time! In our ministry to students throughout the country, we often host question/answer forums and allow the students to ask us any question about any area of life. It just so happens that this one topic comes up every time. Also, students often approach us after we preach to ask for personal advice. Usually, we can guess with remarkable accuracy what the student wants to talk about without knowing anything about the student's life...it's truly amazing! One solitary issue, dominating the minds and hearts of millions...

Of course, the issue is relationships, hence the witty title of our book. The scenario is all too familiar, the sequence is all too predictable: boy has hormones, girl has hormones, boy meets girl, boy likes girl, girl pretends she doesn't like boy, then decides she does, now he doesn't like her...5,741 phone conversations and three hundred emails later, they decide to be "just friends". Until the next day. Now they're holding hands, and talking about getting married one day...she's picking out wedding dresses, he's dreaming of the honeymoon, together they're picking out names for their future goldfish. Until next week, when they break up...kind of...they'll get back together over the weekend. Would someone please STOP THE DRAMA!?!

Do you see why we had to write this book? Sure, there are other books on this subject. We're not being revolutionary here. But we have something to say. We believe God intends for you to guard your heart. We believe He intends for you to find your greatest fulfillment in a living, growing relationship with Him. We also believe that you can't experience that relationship fully if your life is consumed with emotional drama, ungodly flirtation, sexual sin, and all of the destructive consequences that result from ungodly views of love and wrong patterns of dating.

This book is our effort to help you. It is the product of our personal mistakes, successes, stomachaches, and heartbreaks. It is also the product of thousands of hours of counseling and ministering to students and adults. Most importantly, this work is the product of years of Bible study. The principles in this book are tested and true. They are God's ideas about pure and lasting relationships, not our personal opinions. If we've done our job, this book will make you take a deep look at yourself and your views and habits regarding relationships. Some of you will not like what you see. You are in danger of wasting the most foundational years of your life and making some of the most costly mistakes a person can make. This is serious business. Others of you will be encouraged to know that you're not the only one doing it God's way, and you'll find this book practical and reaffirming. We will all be challenged as we confront the desire of every heart: relationships without regret.

The chapters of this book are short. If you will spend a few minutes each day with the material, reading one chapter a day for one month, you'll cover it all and have time to process it. We have divided the book into three main sections. Section one is full of stories. The purpose is to illustrate what true love looks like, and what it doesn't look like. You'll laugh and relate as we share stories about ourselves and people who are close to us. This section is designed to motivate you, to encourage you to think about your own story, and how you want it to turn out. Sections two and three are practical. We don't simply want to motivate you to do better, we want to instruct you on how to do better. Ultimately, we want to point you to Jesus, the only one who can give you meaning and satisfaction.

Jesus said that the greatest commandment is to "love the Lord your God with all your heart, and with all your soul, and with all your mind." (Matthew 22:37) That is our great hope for you. As you read, we pray that God would overwhelm your relationship insanities with Christ-centered realities. A wholehearted love for God is the only lasting pursuit. Whether you are thirteen, twenty-two or fifty-eight years old, God's timeless truths as expressed in this book will help you see things as they really are. It will guide you as you search for a relationship without regret.

Section One

Painting the Picture (Chapters 2-9)

A picture is worth a thousand words, and a good story is often worth a thousand instructions and to do lists. This section is filled with stories about us and others who are near and dear to us. We believe often it is easier to illustrate what real love looks like than describe it. In fact, one of the reasons God came to earth in the form of Jesus Christ was to show us what His love looked like clothed in flesh and blood. Our goal in this section is to show you the flesh and blood embodiment of the Biblical principles that constitute real love and relationship without regret.

As you read through this section, we want you to begin to think about your story. How's it shaping up so far? Ultimately, God is the author. But in His sovereignty He allows you to make choices that lead to one another, and little by little, your life story is written. In your journey through the world of love and dating, you're bound to take some hard knocks. You're going to make some mistakes, not just before marriage, but throughout the course of your marriage. However, you don't have to make the life ruining mistakes that so many students make.

A few things to ponder before moving on:

Who would you like for your story to turn out like? Is there an example you can follow?

If you keep approaching love like you're approaching it now, where will you be in 10 years? 20 years? At age 75?

Are you taking active responsibility in ensuring that your story turns out happily to the glory of God? Or are you just floating along, doing whatever feels right, hoping things will turn out okay?

Are you willing to do what it takes to have the kind of story that God wants you to have? Will you make the sacrifices required? Is it worth it to you?

Do you take seriously the fact that all love stories don't end well? (in fact, they usually don't)

Are you thinking in terms of the rest of your life when you consider your story?

Dive into the following pages which chronicle the real stories of real people. We pray that you will get busy living a story that's worth living.

Chapter 2

Two Dorks Tell All

An excellent wife, who can find? For her worth is far above jewels. The heart of her husband trusts in her, And he will have no lack of gain. She does him good and not evil all the days of her life. Proverbs. 31:10-12 (NASB)

Our wives are beautiful. And smart. And kind. And beautiful. And funny. And thoughtful. And beautiful. And godly. And talented. Did we mention that they're beautiful? Yes, we're bragging. And we're amazed. Basically, Clayton and I are two pretty dorky guys. And so to us, the fact that Charie married Clayton, and Holly married me, proves the very existence and grace of God! How did we do it? How did we marry the women of our dreams? We're about to reveal the secrets of our success...

To be honest, we don't deserve our wives. And although our wives aren't perfect (note to our wives: but you're awfully close!) they have certainly exceeded our dreams and expectations. If I would have been able to customize my wife, picking out every physical, emotional and spiritual component of her makeup, I could not have put together a woman as perfect for me as Holly. Clayton feels the same way about Charie. In the next two chapters, Clayton and I will share the stories of meeting and falling in love with our women. In the last chapters of this section our wives will speak about why they love us, (aw...how sweet!) and what they sought in a man to marry. But in this chapter, I want to reflect on a few of the reasons I believe we have such wonderful wives. Whether you're a guy looking for the perfect gal or a young lady praying for the right man to come your way, this will give you some insight.

1. God is good. We've certainly made enough mistakes to disqualify us from earning wonderful wives. And we're not super good looking. We're certainly not rich (we're preachers!) But God loves to give His children good gifts. Psalm 103:6 says the Lord "satisfies your years with good things so that your youth is renewed like the eagle." The greatest gift He's ever given me other than the gift of His Son Jesus Christ is my wife. God loves you deeply, and He wants to give you good things. Many people seem to believe that if they fully submit their lives to God He'll make them marry somebody who's ugly, smells funny and has an obnoxious laugh. We two dorks disagree! God, in His goodness, gave us women who are attractive to us, fun to be with, wise, and Christ-like.

2. We didn't settle. In later chapters we'll speak more specifically about what you should look for in a spouse. For now, think about this: Proverbs 31:10, our key verse for this chapter, doesn't say "a decent wife who can find."

Anybody can find a boyfriend or a girlfriend. Anyone of legal age can sign a few documents and enter into a marriage relationship. But Proverbs 31:10 states that an excellent wife is hard to find. Clayton and I both had many girlfriends and romantic interests before we met our wives. And we had many opportunities to compromise our standards concerning the kind of women we wanted to marry. I'm not implying that God only has one person you can marry, and if you mess that up your life is ruined and the entire universe is out of balance. However, I often look at my wife, or think about how perfect she is for me, and I'm glad that God's grace kept me from settling for less than God's best for my life. Unless God has called you to be single for the rest of your life, you can bet that He has an unbelievable plan that will blow your mind concerning the person you will marry. These two dorks didn't settle for the passing pleasures of sin or pretty decent wives. Our wives are excellent, and their "worth is far above jewels."

    3. The 6:33 rule. I'm referring to Matthew 6:33, which says that we should *"seek first His Kingdom and His righteousness, and all these things will be added to us."* We were both actively serving and seeking God, and our paths naturally intersected with the paths of our wives, who were also serving and seeking God. Take it from the two dorks: seek God first, let Him be your matchmaker. He's good at it! I look back on the times in my life when I allowed the dating insanity to dominate my thoughts and order my priorities. I know it doesn't make sense, but it wasn't until I quit looking for a wife that I found one! I'm not saying to lock yourself in a room and wait for God to drop a hottie out of the sky. You have a responsibility to respond to God's initiative (more on this later), and there's nothing wrong with the desire for romance. In fact, God put the desire there. We are not anti-dating. We are anti-drama. Anti-impurity. Anti-idolatry (which is putting anything, even good things, before your relationship with the Lord.) Let Christ be your life, and trust Him to fulfill the desires that He gave you. He knows what He's doing.

    Sure there are other reasons our wives love us: our amazing intellectual giftedness, our gentle charm and striking good looks...stop laughing, it's not funny!

    Seriously, I've explained to you three attitudes and paradigms that God has honored in the lives of these two flawed, normal guys. He's blessed us with wonderful wives. This isn't a sure fire formula to get a wife that cooks like Martha Stewart and looks better than Halle Berry. It's not a foolproof plan for you ladies to snag a guy who looks like a cross between Tom Cruise and Brad Pitt and has the spiritual integrity of Billy Graham. It's our story. We're two dorks who are grateful for our wives. God has proven Himself faithful to us, and He'll do the same for you. That's the secret we want to let you in on from the beginning of your journey through this book. That's the secret we want you to remember when sexual temptation is strong. It's the secret we want you to cling to when you feel like you'll be lonely forever. This secret will give you joy when it seems like everyone except you has someone to love, or when your emotions cry out against what you know to be God's reality. The secret is: God is faithful. As you align yourself with His Word and focus on knowing Him, He faithfully blesses your life. Even when you make bad decisions and fall out of line with His will, He will faithfully bless your life as you repent and continue to seek Him. Depend on the faithfulness of God. These two dorks are living proof that He can do anything!

Chapter 3

My Magical Ring (Steven's Story)

Therefore let him who thinks he stands take heed that he does not fall. No temptation has overtaken you but such as is common to man; and God is faithful, who will not allow you to be tempted beyond what you are able, but with the temptation will provide the way of escape also, so that you will be able to endure it.
1 Corinthians 10:12-13 (NASB)

My wedding ring has magical powers. Ok, it's not magical, but it's very special. When my wife Holly was thirteen years old, she pledged to God, her parents, and her future husband (that's me, folks) that she would save herself sexually until marriage. Many chumps, scrubs, and other assortments of guys were interested in Holly throughout her teenage years, and she had the occasional boyfriend here and there. But God, by His grace, kept her sexually pure through it all, and when we married each other on June 1, 2002, we were both virgins. In the weeks before our wedding Holly kept telling me, "You're going to love your wedding ring...you're going to be so proud of your wedding ring..." and I kept thinking, "A ring's a ring, right? It can't be that special. What, does it glow in the dark? Does it give me supernatural heroic powers? Can I look into it and see the future? Will it allow me to travel back in time and roam the earth with the dinosaurs?" On our wedding day, the mysterious ring was revealed. At first glance, the ring looks like a normal gold wedding band. But if you look closely, there is a small stone inserted in the center of the ring. It is the same stone that Holly's parents gave her as a signal of her purity before God when she was thirteen. She had the stone set in my wedding band to remind me forever that she saved herself for me, that she was giving herself to me, and I was worth the wait. A special ring indeed.

Maybe you've made a pledge like Holly did, whether through a True Love Waits campaign or something similar. If you have established a sexual purity covenant, how's it going? I hope you've been victorious thus far, faithfully living out the promises you made to your parents, God, and your future spouse. If you have, praise God for His strength and power, and remain alert. Our key passage for this chapter begins with a serious warning: "Let him who thinks he stands take heed that he does not fall." So rejoice if you're winning the battle against impurity, but stay on your guard. On the other hand, I have met countless students who feel tremendous guilt because they signed commitment cards and failed to keep their commitment. Nothing causes deeper shame for a Christian than the feeling that you've let God down. Perhaps as you read this book, and as you reflect on the stories of God's blessings on our lives, you feel that the sins you've committed or the sin pattern you're presently stuck in eliminates you from God's best for your life. Maybe you've never even taken vows concerning purity because you've not had the opportunity, or you're scared of what will happen if you don't live up to your intentions.

This book is not for perfect people. The Christian life is not for perfect people. It is for desperate people who have come to the end of themselves. It is for humble people who know they can't possibly withstand the incredible temptations of life without Jesus Christ. If you can't shake the feeling that you've "let God down", perhaps I should remind you that you were never holding God up to begin with! And the happy ending/pure beginning that Holly and I celebrated on our wedding day can be your happy ending/pure beginning too. 1 John 1:9 says that "If we confess our sins, He is faithful and righteous to forgive us our sins and to cleanse us from all unrighteousness." As you turn from your sin and turn to Christ, He begins the process of giving you a new start for your future and a fresh perspective on your present reality. Today can literally be a new day for you if you are willing to surrender yourself fully to the Lord.

I'm delving into the specifics of God's available forgiveness and mercy in this chapter because I don't want you to become discouraged by the triumphant stories we share, thinking that you've already ruined your chance to be a pure man or woman of God. Nor do I want to portray that we did things perfectly. I want to be real with you, and the reality is that a relationship without regret brings great reward. When I look at my wedding band and remember that my wife resisted temptation and kept herself for me, I don't regret doing it God's way and keeping myself for her. God's way brings great reward. The fact that Holly isn't mentally comparing me with other sexual partners from her past is a great reward. The fact that I don't have to lay awake at night and wish I'd never given a piece of myself to many different women is a great reward. The pleasure of God and the ability to be a living testimony to His grace is the greatest reward.

I often hear people misquote 1 Corinthians. 10:13 by saying "God won't put more on you than you can bear." That's not what the verse says, and it's not what the context refers to. The Scripture concludes that God, in His faithfulness, will not allow you to be tempted beyond what you are able to bear. That doesn't mean the temptation won't come. In fact, it implies that the temptation will come. But God will provide a way of escape. When I look at my magical wedding band, I'm reminded that God is faithful. He was faithful to my wife, He was faithful to me, and He continues to be faithful to us in our very young marriage. Do you truly believe that God is faithful and able to rescue you from sexual sin? Deep down, are you convinced that God is bigger than your relationship drama? You don't need a magical ring to persuade you of God's faithfulness. His Word, His creation, and His work in your personal life and the lives of those around you are more than sufficient to demonstrate that He is absolutely capable of keeping you pure.

Perhaps you're just not convinced that it's worth it. After all, there are many short term benefits to the dating insanity. There are temporary physical pleasures (more on this in a later chapter). There are social payoffs: it seems that some people like you more when you're dating a certain guy or girl. Personally, I don't need friends like that. There are emotional thrills. And the list could go on with reasons why most students don't approach relationships God's way. It just seems too hard. But as I type this chapter, I just caught a glimpse of my magical wedding ring out of the corner of my eye. And I'm more convinced than ever that doing it God's way is not too hard. What's hard is living a life of regret. What's hard is giving your young heart away to so many different people that you have no idea what real love looks like later in your life. What's truly hard is developing patterns of sexual addiction during adolescence that you have to fight against for the rest of your life. God's way makes sense. It's rewarding. It's available. It's real. It's wonderful. And no matter what you've done or how you feel, it can begin for you right now.

Chapter 4

Clayton's Story, Love At First Blunder

He who finds a wife finds what is good and receives favor from the Lord. Proverbs 18:22 (NIV)

I admit that I do not believe in luck, and that is significant considering the way many things have turned out in my life. To call my journey up until this point "interesting" or "unbelievable" would be a drastic understatement equal to saying "The Titanic took on a little water." I was chased by the KGB in Moscow, Russia. I thought I was going to die of malaria in Kenya, Africa. I was made the King of a village in the Himalayas, and I saw God raise a baby from the dead on a mission trip. But of all the unpredictable and inexplicable things that have occurred in my young life, the most amazing is how I met my wife. It could not possibly be luck. It had to be God.

The year was 1997 and I had just ended a four year relationship with a girl that I sincerely cared about, and had even hoped to marry one day. It was the day after Valentine's and I had sworn off the female race forever while in the throes of heartbreak and loneliness on what was supposed to be the most romantic day of the year.

So the day after Cupid comes to visit so many "twitterpated" hearts (Bambi reference), I found myself at the University of North Carolina at Chapel Hill, home of the Tarheels. I was to speak that night to over 3,000 college students from all over the state of North Carolina at an event called "Forest Fire." I arrived early, had a bite to eat with a friend, and found a seat in the bleachers. I sat and relaxed, thought about my sermon, reflected on the last four years, questioned if I had done the right thing by breaking up with my ex, and watched people enter Carmichael gymnasium.

I was daydreaming, praying, and being entertained by the various stripes and types of college students who wafted in, everything from preps to athletes to hippies. Then, all of a sudden (and this is EXACTLY how it happened), I saw a young lady sitting to my left, slightly above me, about four rows away. She was wearing khaki pants and a white shirt. She was in the process of stooping down to pick up her Bible and backpack. I had never seen her before. I did not recognize her in any way. But at that very split second, I spoke out loud, completely unaware of what I was saying or doing. Before I knew it, I blurted out "Please don't leave!" Then I immediately covered my mouth with my hand in unbelief and surprise. Evidently she did not hear me, and it is a good thing too, because my request was reminiscent of a childish whimper.

I was embarrassed, but smitten. I lost her in the crowd and immediately began an intense prayer vigil before God. I implored Him to please let me find her, talk to her, look at her, just be near her. I became very spiritual and told God if it was His will for us to get married, that He would magnificently draw her to me that night in some way, and that there would be a spark of attraction on her part because I was past "spark" and was moving towards" inferno."

After some music and testimonies, it was my time to preach. I stood before thousands of students for forty-five minutes looking for this mystery woman. I can usually concentrate on multiple things at once. It is simply called Attention Deficit Disorder. I scanned the participants, row-by-row, seat-by-seat. No girl. No luck. I then became cynical and bitter, informing God that it was just Satan trying to tempt me. I was never going be get married because I was going to live for Jesus whole-heartedly, and a woman would just slow me down. I was a member of the P.A.U.L club (Partners Against Uniting with Ladies). I was going to be a He-Man-Woman-Hater like Spanky and Alfalfa of the Little Rascals. I would not fall for a Darla!

God moved that night in a big way. Almost 100 people made decisions for Christ. It was an incredible night for ministry, but I was still a bit shaken from the female sighting and the unusual way this stranger made me feel.

In my sermon, I mentioned that I had started a youth camp called Crossroads and we still needed to hire a few college students for summer staff. I told them if they were interested, to come see me after the event. So when we dismissed, there was a crowd of students assembled, and we were talking about the decisions they had made, the next step for them as Christians, and different things they would be dealing with. Then, all of a sudden without warning, out of nowhere, she appeared.

It was as if God had parted the Red Sea waters and through them emerged a shining specimen of feminine beauty. The crowd split evenly and the mystery girl walked toward me. She struck me as humble yet confident, unimpressed by me or by my sermon. I was stricken with fear. What if my breath stinks? What if I spit on her when I talk? What if I say the wrong thing? One out of three ain't bad.

She walked right up to me, looked me in the eyes, and said clearly "So, you need some help at your summer camp?" I could not believe this was happening to me! Then, in true masculine fashion, I began to talk. Very seldom do men say the right thing, or even the thing they mean to say. I meant to say, "Yes, we need a rock climbing instructor." That was easy enough. No problem, a simple statement. But I was so dumbfounded by the mystery girl that I felt like the world was spinning in slow motion and I sounded like Charlie Brown's teacher on the Peanuts. What I said was "Yeah, we need some help, but probably not you because we need help in SKILL POSITIONS." I could not believe what I had just said. I was doomed.

I tried to bail out, but it was too late. There was nothing that I could say, and if I ventured more words, they would have definitely been to my detriment. Then, as if nothing out of the ordinary happened, mystery girl responded with grace and confidence with "What skills are you talking about because I have experience in rock climbing, rappelling, white water rafting, and caving."

I was speechless, flabbergasted, whopper jawed, taken aback, and utterly surprised. Not only was she not impressed with me, she was so secure and confident that she was not even offended by my verbal blunder. My unfortunate response would have hurt some girl's feelings, angered others, and even devastated a few. But this girl took it in stride without any evidence of discomfort or misunderstanding. I was now officially impressed and dare I even say it, in love?

She did apply to Crossroads, and she was hired (shocker!). Little did I know that at about the same time I broke off a long-standing relationship, she broke off an engagement. We were both recovering and being restored to sanity after the emotional trauma of hard break-ups. Neither was in search of the next relationship. Quite the opposite! We had both decided the whole dating debacle was for the younger stallions of stronger heart and constitution, but not us. I had actually decided to take six months and go on a dating and girl fast of sorts so that I could focus on Christ and ministry and being the kind of person Jesus wanted me to be. I did not want the distraction and awkwardness of getting to know someone new, dating, playing the whole silly little game again. So for the next five to six months, we did not flirt or date or hold hands or kiss. We had no late night conversations. We just prayed and sought God, both of us oblivious to the fact that the other person was attracted to us. We simply did not pursue the relationship in our flesh. We waited on God and kept our cool. It went slow. I had her staff picture on my nightstand beside my bed, and I would stare at it for hours, praying for God's will. But I never told her. I wanted God to do this if it was to be done at all. We were two hours driving distance apart and living different lives but praying for each other.

Crossroads started and the very night that I had decided to tell her about my feelings and intentions, she beat me to the punch. She approached me, literally, 30 seconds before I had decided to confess my love for her and said, "I need to know how you feel about me, because I have feelings for you. And if you don't have feelings for me, tell me, because I don't want to keep hanging on to hope if you are not the one God has for me. I don't want to waste time on the wrong person. But if you do have feelings, and I hope you do, I would like to know." I responded in something about as intelligent and romantic as Jim Carey in Dumb and Dumber. It came out kinda like "Um, I like you a lot?"

We waited till the summer was over, and the last day of Crossroads in front of 500 students, I gave her a dozen roses on stage and asked her to be my girlfriend. We already loved each other, but we patiently waited on God to bring things to pass as opposed to frantically sprinting ahead of Him. It paid off, too.

We dated for almost two years. I paid cash for a diamond that I had saved for since the day we started dating and I took her to Gingercake Mountain in Linville Gorge, NC (where Last of the Mohicans was filmed). I proposed to her at a spot where I had been five years earlier, snowed in on a camping trip. I sat there in the white wilderness, dreaming about my future wife, writing about her in my journal, and said to myself "I think this is the place I will pop the question one day." All those dreams came true, and she said yes. Six months later, we tied the knot at the Green River Plantation (our wedding day is another story, or book, in and of itself).

So when people ask me if I believe in love at first sight, I tell them yes and no. Then I relay my own story. I fell in love with Charie at first sight, but I choose to believe that she fell in love with me at first blunder. How about that! She married me in spite of who I am, and look at the deal I got!

So you see, I do not believe in luck, because a man could never be as lucky as me. It had to be Divine Providence coupled with God's sympathy for a young country boy who just could not do or say the right thing. I am glad he decided to bail me out, and that she decided not to bail out on me. Lucky me? No, blessed me!

Chapter 5

A Success Story by Steven

But now faith, hope, love, abide these three; but the greatest of these is love. 1 Corinthians 13:13 (NASB)

In the months before I married Holly, I kept a notebook in which I recorded all the marriage advice people gave me. I asked almost everyone I respected, and even some complete strangers on airplanes to share with me the most important marriage tips they could think of. The responses ranged from brilliant to idiotic, from gravely serious to extremely sarcastic. Here's a sample of the what people said:

"Don't do it boy!"
"Only two words you need to know: Yes Ma'am"
"Pray and read scripture together every single day" (a practice we've worked hard to incorporate thus far)
"Listen to your wife, she's smarter than you"
"Never stop winning her heart"

The list goes on, but by far the most treasured piece of advice was given by my grandfather shortly before he went to be with the Lord:

"You just hang in there no matter what."

Overly simplistic? Idealistic? In my opinion, more profound and timely words were never spoken. In this chapter, I want to give you an inside look at true love that hangs in there no matter what. You may ask what my grandparents' marriage has to do with your love life. My goal is to show you a picture of true love. The kind of love that doesn't rise and fall with feelings, and that isn't dependent on hormonal thrills or outward beauty. Hopefully by seeing this picture, you'll have a clearer understanding of what true love is...and what it is not. And that correct view of lasting real love will become the framework for a relationship without regret in your own life.

I won't bore you with many autobiographic details about Grandma and Papa. The meat of it is: they married young and raised two children, Tommy and Faith (my mother). Papa was a Methodist preacher most of his adult life, Grandma was a professional educator and the consummate preacher's wife. I'm sure a survey of the earlier years of their marriage would provide many object lessons on love, but I wasn't around then. I only really observed the last decade of their marriage, and from a natural perspective it was a tragic ending. From the perspective of God's idea of love it was a grand finale.

About ten years ago, Grandma was diagnosed with Alzheimer's Disease. If you've ever watched a loved one struggle with this brutal illness, you know that it progresses little by little until, in most cases, the victim literally loses his or her mind. For the last six years of her life, Grandma lived in a constant state of terror and confusion. She often awoke in the middle of the night in a cold sweat, scared to death that an intruder was in the house. She didn't know who I was, she didn't recognize her children, and eventually she couldn't even identify her own husband, who came to visit her in the nursing home every single day without fail. Papa woke up early in the morning, drove to the facility, and sat all day long with a woman who generally didn't know who he was. Papa had developed a little daily routine which was their custom until their health prevented them from getting around: He sat by her side at the nursing home all morning, and at 11:30 on the dot they patronized the local Wendy's fast food restaurant, where the workers knew them by name. Since they ordered the same meal every day, they didn't even have to tell the cashier what they wanted; it was the same three items from the 99 cent value menu (Papa was quite the cheapskate) with one medium Diet Pepsi, which they shared, every single day. After sitting in Wendy's for two or three hours watching the people (something old folks seem to love to do), they'd head back to the nursing home until visiting hours were over and the staff kicked Papa out. He'd be back the next morning, bright and early, to do it all again.

Eventually, Grandma's health deteriorated so badly that even these simple trips to Wendy's were impossible. Her mental faculties eventually eroded so severely that she didn't recognize simple objects like a spoon or a fork. Papa watched his once bright and beautiful bride lose her ability to think, speak coherently, or even use the restroom. When she did speak to him, it was to curse him and tell him how much she hated him. She literally had no more control of her emotions, and all logical thought had eluded her. None of this ever stopped Papa from enduring hour upon hour in the Alzheimer's wing of the assisted living home, brushing his wife's hair, telling her how beautiful she was.

As I grow up, I marvel more every day at the love that enabled Papa to love his wife in those last few agonizing years of their marriage. It was a love that compelled him to sit with her in a cold, depressing nursing home for eight hours a day, even though she wasn't completely aware of his presence, and she certainly wouldn't remember that he'd been there. It was a love that was demonstrated again and again by the way he gently spoke to her and told her he loved her regardless of her ability to reciprocate his affection. This love outlasted the jitters and butterflies that accompany newfound romance. It was not dependent on external beauty; it did not rise and fall with the ebb and flow of life.

1 Corinthians 13, that famous chapter cited at most Christian weddings, describes this true love. Paul calls love patient, kind, humble, and a score of other things that run much deeper than surface emotions. And the chapter

concludes by extolling love over all the other virtues, implying that it is the only thing that will live forever. Are you ready for real love? The kind of love that demanded of my grandfather that he comb the hair of his wife as she stared blankly into space, not even knowing he was there? Are you ready for that? Or are your prayers for true love really just fantasies of your emotional and physical needs being met?

The reason so many marriages don't last is because most individuals don't have a completely functional understanding of love. 1 Corinthians 13, along with the example of my Papa, have provided me with a foundation on which I'm building my lifelong relationship with my wife. What does this mean for you as you pray, date and develop in preparation for marriage? You'd better be prepared to "hang in there no matter what." You should approach each opportunity for relationship with caution and a long term perspective. It is disheartening to me to see students enter the pattern of dating...breaking up...dating someone else...breaking up....I am concerned that this cycle develops a poor pattern for the relationship of marriage. The devastating results are evidenced by the alarming de-emphasis on the sanctity of marriage in today's "if it doesn't work out, give up and try somebody else" society. God's idea of marriage is hanging in there, no matter what. His idea of love is 1 Corinthians 13. His demonstration of love was most vividly expressed on a cruel cross, giving His own life for us "while we were still sinners" (Romans 5:8).

Papa died about a year and a half before Grandma. Just before Papa died, I was driving him around town one day and I asked him, "How do you do it? How do you give yourself to Grandma every day, expecting nothing in return?" He looked at me as if my question wasn't worth answering. To him the answer was implicit and obvious: "She's my wife." Enough said. Papa had determined to finish what he started. The grace of God enabled him to do so. A few years ago, in a rare moment of clear thought, Grandma told me something about Papa I'll never forget. Her words were slow and slurred, but their impact changed my life. We were eating at Wendy's (of course) when she looked me in the eye, pointed to Papa, and said, "That's a good man. He loves me no matter what. Aggravates the fool out of me sometimes, but loves me no matter what." A relationship without regret requires real love. A love that "hangs in there no matter what." Settle for nothing less.

Chapter 6

Clayton: Finish What You Started

When a man makes a vow to the Lord or takes an oath to obligate himself by a pledge, he must not break his word but must do everything he said. Numbers 30:2 (NIV)

When Steven and I sat down one afternoon for three hours at the Snack Shop in Boiling Springs and hammered out the basic structure and outline of this book, we felt it would be advantageous to spend a bit of time highlighting some success stories in relationships. Since the ultimate goal of romantic relationships is a lifetime of marriage, the only applicable success story, in my estimation, would be one of a married couple. Not puppy love or middle school dramas, but the big plunge of marriage without looking back. So I began to run through the list of married people I know.

I think of Wilkes and Mary Skinner. He was my pastor when I was saved who allowed me to speak at Crossroads Baptist Church as a fourteen year old with no experience. He gave me a safe place to hone a skill and make mistakes. He was faithful to his family when one son was tragically killed as a teenager. He had a daughter who never developed mentally or emotionally and had to live in an assisted living facility for her whole life. But the greatest example was his faithfulness to Mary, his wife, when she was diagnosed with bone marrow cancer and spent nearly two years in Washington State getting a marrow transplant. He stayed by her side and sent cassette tapes each week to our congregation that we listened to every Sunday morning. He never blinked or missed a moment of service to her or his family.

I think of Mr. And Mrs. Hawks at Pleasant Grove. I dare say there is not a sweeter, kinder couple on earth. Though in their twilight years in this life, they still hold hands as they walk across the parking lot at church. They both greet me with a kiss and ask how the ministry is going when I see them. They never complain about the numerous things they could gripe about, but instead choose to be cheerful, encouraging, and loving. They survived a depression, a World War, the turbulence of the 1960's, and they never blinked or flinched in their love for one another.

There is also the young man I met many years ago who told me how he found out the day before he had planned to propose to his girlfriend that she was dying with terminal cancer. Against all advisors, he asked anyway. She said yes, and they spent exactly two months together as husband and wife before she left this world. Her sickness made it impossible for them to be physically intimate, but he said two months with her was better than never being with her at all.

Oh, you could name successes, too. These are the kind of stories that make people feel warm and fuzzy and that make Oprah famous. They are the stories that country music songs are written about.

Everyone desires, I believe, to belong to someone, just one, for a lifetime without worry or doubt. It is that unshakable, consistent confidence that no matter what transpires there is a mate, a partner in your life that will never leave your side. Movies can be made about romantic interludes, but families and legacies are carved from lives spent navigating shaky seas and dangerous waters together.

It is with these things in mind that I reflect on the couple I know best that just so happens to encapsulate all the ups and downs of marriage with a firm dedication to never quit. They could have, and in many opinions should have, thrown in the towel long ago and numerous times. Instead they took their marriage vows as real vows and not hollow words.

My mama and daddy.

Joe King was born poor, really. World War II was ending, and in rural SC you lived off what you could grow and what you could kill. His daddy, my grandaddy, left his wife and three children when my daddy was only ten years old. He told me that he would sit at the window as a boy for hours waiting on his father to come home, but he never did. There were times during those lean years that neighbors would bring food to their house and it would be the only thing they had to eat all day. No running water, just an outhouse and a well with a bucket. No hot shower, just a tin tub with hot water warmed on the stove every Saturday night before church on Sunday. Daddy was loading boxcars with fertilizer sacks as a little boy, and his brother and sister had to pitch in, too. He said they did not know they were poor because everyone else was in the same shape as they were. There was even a time he wanted to play on the basketball team but did not have shoes to wear. Not just basketball shoes, but shoes period.

Jane Knight was raised poor, too. She was born while her daddy, a Cherokee Indian, was serving in the South Pacific on a Navy vessel during WWII. She was scared of him when she first saw him at nearly four years of age because she did not know him. Their house was an old chicken coop. They got water from a fresh water spring that I played in as a boy, and they brought it to the house in buckets. Her mama loved to work a garden and labored to keep food on the table, while Papa, who loved to drink, wasted the paycheck away on liquor. But boy, could he play bluegrass! Just like the legends; Flatts and Scruggs and Monroe. There was never any money, and my mother was their only child.

Joe and Jane met and fell in love as teenagers and married young. There was no seed money or inheritance. They lived in mama's childhood bedroom until they could build their own house. They both knew how to work so that is what they did. Mama worked as a secretary and daddy worked his way from sweeping the floors at an electric motor shop to owning that shop.

They could not conceive so they adopted two boys; me and my younger brother Brad. They instilled in us the same work ethic they were taught. Though I hated the chores of feeding animals, plowing and picking, splitting wood and sweeping floors, I thank God every single day now for those lessons. We were taken to church. We cleaned our plates. We ate meals at a table, together, as a family. We prayed before we ate and talked after we were finished. We played outside. Daddy came home each day after work and never deviated from his routine. Mama did without clothes and jewelry and vacations so we could have shoes and pants for school. My sweetest childhood memories are of sitting on the porch on hot summer nights listening to my family play and sing gospel and bluegrass and of me and daddy getting up before daylight and loading the dogs up to go hunting. Walking beside him as the sun broke the horizon made me feel like I had something to live towards. I had an example to follow. He knew the way.

As the years have passed, all of my grandparents have died. I have preached two of their funerals. Another generation is gone with nothing but fading photographs and memories. Now my parent's health has begun to fail. Their minds are sharp but their bodies are beginning to bend under the weight of time and mileage. Mama has had multiple surgeries and a stroke. Daddy has had two heart attacks. He is diabetic. He has sleep apnea. He has high blood pressure and chemical imbalances, and the list could fill up this page for them both.

Yet just two days before writing these words, I looked out my window at 6:30 one morning to see what my dog was barking at, and it was my daddy who had come to bring me some fresh tomatoes and cantaloupes he had grown for me. He said he just missed me and decided he would drive the sixty-two miles to our house to see us. Mama spends most of her days thinking and worrying about her children and grandchildren. When I was called into the ministry, they supported and encouraged me to go. They came to the airport when I left for Russia, Africa, and India. Mama washed my practice uniform every night during football season for twelve years and cooked every meal that we men ate until we left home. She still cooks every meal for daddy. Tonight I bet they had black-eyed peas, cornbread, and milk.

They gave me what I pray someone gives you. They gave me an example. It was not a pretty one. It was not a perfect one. But it was real, practical, authentic, and genuine. They fought and lost their tempers at times, but they stuck it out, and sometimes maybe even just for our sake. Imagine that! Parents who do the right thing for their children regardless of what might make them happy for the moment.

They gave me what I pray someone gives you. They gave me a legacy. I want to see my son watching me and Charie grow in years and in love for each other. I want to tell my children about my parents and be proud. I want to pass on a name and I want my son to feel the same sense of worth and purpose that I felt when I would try to step in my daddy's footprints in the dirt when we were planting summer corn.

They gave me what I pray someone gives you. They gave me memories. Good and bad. Painful and pleasant. But they are mine. I knew that daddy was coming home after work and that mama would pick me up from school. I knew that when they said thanks for their food, it meant something because they had experienced hunger in their lives. Their unwavering consistency has become for me a catalog of memories, of hearing my father yell for me at a T-ball game and seeing mama in the stands on Friday night before I started as linebacker on varsity football. Trips to the hospital. Visits to the funeral home. Sitting together as a family at church. Catching a stringer full of bass and cleaning them, then eating them the same day for lunch. There was nothing flashy about it. Some would even say that I was raised redneck or white trash. Well, you call it what you want, but I would trade every SUV, every resort vacation, all the fancy clothes and big parties for those humid August nights, crickets chirping and fireflies buzzing, sitting on my mama's lap listening to daddy play his guitar and sing "The Green, Green Grass of Home." You know, they are right. There are some things that money just can't buy.

Chapter 7

What Went Wrong?

But everyone who hears these words of mine and does not put them into practice is like a foolish man who built his house on sand. The rain came down and the streams rose and the winds blew and beat against that house, and it fell with a great crash.
Matthew 7:26-27 (NIV)

The statistics tell us that today, for every success story in marriage, there are two failures. I would guess there is no reliable statistic for how many dating relationships end up in failure, but it would be a safe bet to say "most."

Have you ever thought about what you are doing when you date someone? When you flirt a little bit? When you break up with someone to go out with someone else?

There are only two possibilities for each relationship you have.
Ultimately.
Two.
That is it. No other possibility exists beyond these two.
I dare you to even think of another possibility. You can't do it.
You will get married...
Or...
You will break up.
Period.

Now don't give me that "We will still be friends" bit, because you still have to break up to get there. There are only two options in the end. You marry or you break it off. It is like being pregnant. You either are or you are not.

So many relationships and marriages end up on the rocks, broken and busted due to any number or circumstances. Money, jealousy, family, cheating, lack of communication, materialism, lies, you name it. It is all of the things that make a successful TV drama or sitcom. The more dysfunctional a relationship, the more likely we are as a culture to be fixated upon it. Go figure.

The sad thing is, when writing a chapter on "What Went Wrong" I have so many examples to choose from that I have a hard time picking one. It seems to be the norm today, just sign out of marriage or a relationship with the same painless ease as signing out of class at school.

I feel scared to talk about this because I don't want to come across as flippant or judgmental on this subject. It could happen to me too. I am not above sin, nor am I perfect in any way. And I still pray and believe that this couple will one day repent and be reconciled and reunited. I chose a couple that no one would possibly know, and I chose them for the sheer brutality of their situation as a warning to you. Do not build on sand. Be careful. Be cautious. Be patient. And be sure.

I was very close to this married couple and their three young children. I spent the night in their home, and I even slept in their son's room when I was traveling through town on my way to preach. He would sleep with his sisters, and my feet would hang off the end of his bed. I played in the yard with them, watched Mr. Rogers with them, and they dog piled me every time I came to visit. But I began to notice mom and dad acting different. At first I ignored it, but it became more obvious as time went on. I asked the dad about it. He blew it off saying they were both really tired. I asked the mom about it and she dismissed it by saying they were just both really busy. That sounded normal enough.

Then one day their little boy asked me why his mom and dad hated each other. I asked why he thought that, and he said they never talked unless they were mad at each other. So I went back again and asked them how they were. They both lied and said fine. I knew they were lying, but what else could I do? I even told them I knew they were lying. Shortly thereafter I got the word that he had left and they were separated. I tracked him down and asked him if he was addicted to pornography, because in my experience with marriages that go wrong, many times porn is at the root. He categorically denied it. Then I asked if he had had an affair, and he denied that as well. He blamed her. I spoke with her over the phone and asked her if she had been unfaithful. She assured me she had not, but that they had just drifted apart over the years. The spark was gone and they were no longer in love with each other. Then she told me that they had stayed together all that time for the kids and they finally deserved to be happy, so they were going to get divorced. They both informed me this would be best for the kids, too.

To me, this was reprehensible, but for many it is just par for the cultural course. I told them both that as Christians, divorce was a last resort and that God wanted them to repent and reconcile to each other, for themselves, their children, and for their faith as Believers in Christ. Both were unwilling.

The divorce went through. It was ugly and uncivil. The children were torn apart. When the dust cleared and the days turned to years, an interesting thing unfolded before my eyes. Their two girls became cynical and angry. As they matured, they began to dress extremely immodestly. The guys they dated had terrible reputations. Rumors about their drinking and partying circulated. One girl became pregnant while the other became a cutter and drug-addict.

The son rebelled in every conceivable way. He got in trouble with the law. He was expelled from two schools. He eventually dropped out. I bumped into him when he was about seventeen and had a depressing conversation. I simply asked him, "What went wrong with you?" His two-word response was "My parents."

I saw one of his sisters at Wal-Mart one day and asked her, "What Went

Wrong?" She said, "Ever since mom and dad split up, I haven't really given a @#&* about anything."

Then, after several years, I had a chance to spend several hours with the dad. After the small-talk, I just asked him if we could quit being fake and talk about the 800-pound gorilla in the room that we both seemed to be trying to ignore. "What Went Wrong?" For some reason, he just opened up and spilled his guts. He had been building on sand all along, and the house finally crashed.

It started when he was twelve. He found pornographic magazines that his dad had hidden, and he became addicted to them. Then it led to movies that he and his buddies would watch on the weekends. When he hit puberty, he said his one desire was to have sex with a girl. He lost his virginity at age fourteen and swore he would never do it again. But he craved it and porn did not satisfy him, so he just began to live for sex. It consumed his thoughts and dreams. He felt guilty but did not know how to stop.

Then he had "an experience with God." He said he was saved, and he thought that would take away the desires, but within a week he had been with another girl. He struggled with guilt and condemnation and thought he would go to hell for it. But he said that he wanted sex more than Jesus, so he quit fighting it. Then he met his wife. He thought if he got married, the temptation would go away. So he married her more for his own selfish desire rather than out of love and desire for her. Unfortunately things did not get better after marriage.

With the availability of filth on the Internet his porn addiction took a severe turn. He began to look at gay porn and had an affair with a man. When his wife found out, she flipped on him and went out and had an affair to get even with him for what he had done to her. For a while after the divorce they thought they had their kids fooled, then they realized that their children had figured out what had happened. Instead of talking to their children, repenting for their sins, and asking their children to forgive them, they decided silence was best. So they never broached the subject. They NEVER even brought it up, even though they both knew that their children were aware of the circumstances. So their kids had no safe place to vent, no safe outlet to express their hurt. They had no one to guide them through the emotional minefield they had to navigate all alone.

Mom and dad both messed up. Both were too proud and stubborn to admit it and ask forgiveness. Both were too lazy and self-centered to attempt the long hard road of reconciliation. Sure the dad started it, but this is not a fight on the playground at recess. We are talking about people's lives. Blame was not the issue. The marriage was built on sand, not rock. It was destined to crumble eventually.

To my knowledge, they still live in different states. The children are still struggling as they approach their twenties. They both have been re-married and divorced. And I still pray that they will one day reconcile.

Do I need to spell out for you what went wrong? They were married too early and for all the wrong reasons. They brought baggage into the marriage that should have been dealt with prior to wedding vows. They perpetuated a lie in front of their children. They lied to friends who saw red flags, and they shunned accountability. They chose not to fight for their marriage and their children and took the most convenient exit route; divorce. They ignored their children and refused to consider their needs. He had addictions as a teenager that ruined his life later. And the list goes on.

Please, I beg you, do not think for a skinny minute that this cannot happen to you. It can and it does, every single day, to people just like you who do not consider the gravity of relationships and the consequences that loom over making stupid decisions.

Be careful.
Be cautious.
Be patient.
Be sure.
Do not build on sand.

Chapter 8

Two Babes Tell All by Holly

By the time I was eighteen years old, I had three criteria for my future husband; I wanted him to be the godliest guy I knew, I wanted him to be my best friend, and I wanted him to be called to the ministry in some way. So being the practical person that I am, I set myself up to find that man when I went away to college. I was not actively seeking him. I was not even looking for a prospect because I knew that relationships take time and that God was in control.

Somewhere along the way, I learned a few key things that I believe set me up to find the man of my dreams. I knew that in order to find a godly man, I needed to be a godly woman. I decided that the most important thing in my life at that time was for me to be grounded in the Word of God. My goal was to know God with all my heart and to love him with my entire being. I had seen and heard of so many Christian girls who went to college and got caught up in the wrong crowd or with the wrong guy. I wanted to prevent this from happening to me, so before I got to college, I made a commitment to the Lord that I would not date anyone for my entire first year of college. The sole purpose of this commitment was to grow closer to the Lord and protect myself from any distractions.

In addition to this commitment, I went about setting myself up for success. I found an accountability partner to challenge me and memorize scripture with me. I sought out friends who were walking with God. No, we did not sit around and have Bible study on Friday nights, but we encouraged each other and had fun doing positive things. These were not all girls, in fact, many of them were guys, but I did not have the intention of dating any of them. I also got involved in a Bible study and regularly attended church and para-church groups on campus. All of these things kept me focused on becoming the person that I needed to be, the person that God wanted me to become. I am not going to say that those "guy friends" didn't have other ideas, but I made it real clear to them that I was not dating anyone for a year and we hand a good time hanging out and developing relationships.

During this time I was busy, involved in ministry on and off campus. I continued to live the life that God had called me to live knowing that eventually, He would bring the right man along. Do not think that this was an easy commitment for me. There were many nights when I was lonely, many times when I felt as though I was the only one who didn't belong to anyone, and many days when I wanted desperately to break my commitment. But during these times, I clung to the Lord, to my commitment to Him and to His Word. I believe that this time of obedience in my life was a time of emotional and spiritual maturity.

This commitment was beneficial to my second criteria. I knew that I wanted to marry my best friend. I also knew that best-friendships are not made over night, in fact, they take months to form. So many girls make the mistake of dating a guy before they even know him. I figured if I knew the guy as a friend I would be able to see if he was godly and if he was the guy for me without having my heart broken if he didn't live up to my expectations.

Wouldn't you know that at freshman orientation, I shook hands with Steven Furtick? He was a silly punk-rocker with a superman shirt and ragged Goodwill corduroys, definitely not my type in the fashion category. As I watched him on campus, it was easy to see his inward character and love for God. Sometime during our first semester, we became friends. We didn't do stuff off campus much (I wasn't into MXPX concerts and mosh pits), but we did eat many meals together in the cafeteria, and we began to spend a lot of time talking on the phone. In January of that year, Steven was asked to lead a summer ministry team sponsored by the college. He accepted the position and set about to find the rest of his five person team. He called and asked me if I would be a part. (Note from Steven: Not a bad idea huh? Trap her into spending the whole summer with me!) After prayer and consideration, I agreed.

That summer was when I found my best friend. I was able to watch Steven respond in a variety of circumstances. I saw how he treated his mom and others under his leadership. I laughed with him and talked with him for hours with no romantic interest. When we went back to school, I realized how comforting he was to me. How he always made me feel welcome in a group of people. He was kind and thoughtful. I wanted to talk with him more than anyone else in my life. Pretty much the rest is history.

Our relationship was built on a friendship, not on a physical relationship. And that is what our relationship is rooted in today. He is and always will be my best friend. I love talking with him, laughing with him, and being with him. I knew him well before we ever started dating and fell in love with him without even realizing it because I waited and was obedient to the Lord.

I wanted to marry a man who walks with God, and I waited patiently with my eyes focused on the Lord. My third criterion was met when I got to see how Steven ministers to others and how he responds under pressure. It was obvious that God had called him into the ministry.

When you seek after something without waiting on the Lord, you will get immediate satisfaction, but you will end up settling for less than God's best for your life. Be the man or woman of God that you want to find in someone else. Spend time getting to know the Lord, and surround yourself with people who will encourage you in your daily walk with the Lord. Do not waste your time "looking" for your future mate in places where godly people do not hang out (clubs, wild parties, etc...), you will only find distractions that could ruin your life. Keep your eyes on the Lord and do the stuff you know He has called you to do now. The rest will fall into place in His time.

Chapter 9

Two Babes Tell All by Charie

When I used to travel with Clayton full-time (before Jacob was born) people used to ask us lots of questions. I especially received a lot of attention from high school girls who wanted to know how to find such a godly man because they could never find any where they lived. I would be asked a variety of questions and statements like: How did you do it? How did you find such a godly man? You guys seem like you really love each other and I can tell you have such a good marriage. How do you know when you meet the right one? What should I look for in a person? I just don't think there is anyone out there for me.

While I think that there are specific things that you can do to avoid hurtful and unhealthy relationships (which is the purpose of this book), I have to be honest in saying that I don't think you can ever have it totally together when it comes to love. Feelings of like and love can really confuse the most well-balanced and God-seeking person on the earth no matter what their age. It is easy to get mixed up. Love is at the root of many people's most rash decisions, most embarrassing moments, most costly investments, as well as the most beautiful commitments in the world.

When I was in elementary school, I definitely had an interesting perspective on a future mate. My experimentation with flirty feelings began with a series of crushes on three boys in Elementary School. All of their names happened to be JASON, and so I felt this was a sign that one day I had to marry someone named Jason. Perhaps this was the most popular male name in my town, but for an elementary student who couldn't stop wishing that Jason T. would sit by her on a field trip, or that Jason W. would share some of his Little Debbie snacks, or that Jason B. would pass me the ball in one of our soccer games, the only conclusion I could come to was that I would one day become Mrs. Jason ******. My entire destiny was devastated when I was tragically attracted to a new boy named JOHN. "Oh no, what will I do?", I thought. Then I concluded, "Well, at least his name starts with a 'J'. Maybe I am just supposed to marry someone with a name that starts with 'J'". Now I am married to Clayton King. Amazingly enough my life was not devastated because his name starts with a "C". In fact, I would rather have Clayton than any man whose name starts with "J".

This story may seem a little "cheezy", and most of the guys reading this are probably saying to themselves, "Are girls really this ridiculous?" Perhaps "all" girls are not, but I did have these thoughts as a young, silly, and dreamy fourth and fifth grader. I believe we all imagine and hope for true love. Perhaps this stems from that deep longing that God places in our hearts to be fully known, and maybe a little of it is based on fairy tales, movies, or true love stories that we have heard from others. No matter where this desire comes from, I know it is so strong that the most grounded person is willing to endure great heartache in order to walk on the clouds of love for awhile.

In my world of dating, I have blundered through a few relationships, while others were handled well; breaking up with no regrets except the pain and hurt from the loss of companionship. After years of being married to my wonderful husband, it becomes easy to forget the reality of being frustrated with wanting to be loved and wanting to love another person in full security. However, with years of marriage I am also able to look back on my dating experiences and offer a little wisdom of things to avoid and things to pursue.

Detrimental Reasons for Dating:

1. I was lonely and wanted to fit in.
2. I had just broken up with someone and was used to having someone around to lean on.
3. I felt pressured. Family and friends would ask me who I was dating and make it seem as if something was wrong if I wasn't going out with someone especially on the weekends.
4. Because I felt bad for the guy who asked me and didn't want to hurt his feelings.
5. Because everyone else would have gone out with him if he had asked them, so I should because everyone else thinks he's a great guy.
6. Because I did not want to graduate college without a man to marry.

Believe me, it is not easy to admit these feelings and shortcomings. And while I did not date many guys throughout high school and college (six total), I learned a lot from each relationship. Some of the guys I dated were truly godly and incredible, and valued me and my relationship with God. In these friendships I learned some valuable positive aspects of dating.

Some of the positive things I learned dating:

1. Staying away from the physical aspects of a relationship is possible and doesn't leave as many regrets. I dated a guy for about two years or more and we never kissed and barely held hands, but we did a lot of really fun activities which I don't mind remembering today.
2. Pray before you get involved, and pay attention to what God says.
3. Keep your parents involved in your dating life and listen to their advice. (I was engaged to a guy and broke it off

because I finally listened to my family. He was a great guy, but we were more in love with being married than each other and my family knew that before I did.)

4. Open communication is hard, but it really helps a relationship in every aspect.

My best dating experience happened the end of my senior year at Appalachian State. I had really been growing in my walk with the Lord that year because it had been so hard and lonely. After my first semester, I broke off an engagement and although my family truly supported me, many of my friends did not. I spent a lot of time alone and God used this to produce a deep-hearted intimacy between He and I. I look back on this time and sincerely treasure the comfort and encouragement the Lord offered me as He slowly repaired my heart. I truly spent each day with the Lord undistracted. I confided in Him, trusted Him, cried to Him, and let Him calm me to sleep. He was my ever-present friend and I truly did not want anyone else to fill that place in my heart.

One day a friend of mine invited me to go to Chapell Hill to a college event called "Forest Fire". I was reluctant because I had to work and it was a two hour drive, but she talked me into it. In the gymnasium, I listened to a man preach who inspired me to continue to be obedient and in love with Jesus. I felt a closeness to him as he spoke that was unexplainable because I had never met him, heard of him, seen him in person or in a picture. He mentioned in his sermon that he was content to be single and serve God for the rest of his life. I was in the same position. I had already told the Lord that I would be willing to travel overseas and be a missionary for a year if He wanted. I was praying about this and two other job opportunities.

As I listened to this man preach, I sensed a sincerity and genuiness in what he shared. He spoke about his trip to India and his love for the people and admiration for their faithfulness in spite of persecution. Because of my longing to go overseas, this really sat deep within my heart. He also said that he was going to India again soon and in my heart I felt myself wish that I could go with him, not only for the missions but also to get to know him a little more. It seemed like he gained my instant respect, but there was also so much hesitation in my heart. I truly believe that the Lord told me I would marry this man that night. This scared me so much that I wanted to run and leave the gym the minute I had marriage on my mind.

After the message the man mentioned that he needed a rock climbing instructor to work at camp, but because I had already wondered if I would marry him and because there was a hoard of people around him, I tried to exit the building. On the way out, I spotted a friend of mine named Molly who chatted with me for a minute and then said she really liked the speaker and could see me marrying him. This scared me once again and I begged her not to say such things. Then, I saw another friend of mine named Eric. He came up to me and said, "OOOOOH girl, let me tell you something. That man up there was the real deal. I can really see the two of you together, and you'd have pretty babies too!" I thought to myself, "What is this? A plot to scare Charie Harper to death."

So, I gave up and decided I would ask him about the camp job. As I walked toward him, there were still a lot of people and I said to myself, "If I get up there and wait for more than three minutes, I'm out of here." So, I proceeded and as I got closer, everyone left. I was nervous by this time, but I said to him, "Hey Clayton, I heard you mention that you still need a rock climbing instructor for camp and I was wondering if I could apply for the position." The rest of this story is in Clayton's chapter of how we met, and he will say that I was all calm and collected. Maybe I seemed that way, but inside I was nervous and not wanting to mess up my emotions again. I am aware that this was the time that God felt was appropriate for our meeting, but I never would have guessed that I would have felt more inhibited and unready for such a time in my life.

We really did not talk to each other much for six months. I simply had a feeling about him and prayed for him. I knew that the Lord was in control and that he would organize the way things should go. We spent a few simple moments together including one cup of hot chocolate with a friend when he spoke at InterVarsity at my school Appalachian, dinner at Backyard Burger when he was traveling through one day, and a day at Carowinds handing out camp brochures. The day at Carowinds sealed the deal. He made me feel more at ease and laugh more than I had laughed in two whole years. I needed to laugh. I needed some fun. I needed to get away, and I needed to feel safe. Clayton made me feel all these things and he still does. We met his parents for dinner that day we went to Carowinds and they accepted me because "I was a girl who wasn't afraid to clean her plate."

Five to six months of prayer about our relationship gave me the confidence and peace that God was in favor of us being together. People always ask "How do you know he is the one?". All I can say is that I JUST KNEW. Another confirmation of our relationship came with the approval of all of my family. This was a great gift to me. I needed to know they were supporting me.

As Clayton and I got to know each other more deeply, I realized that God had given me a gift more wonderful than I had ever imagined. His consistent love amazed me so much that I tried to push it away, but he stayed persistent and faithful to me winning my trust and lifelong loyalty.

My husband is my best friend. I treasure his presence in my life daily. I miss him when he is gone, and I am glad when we get to sleep in the same bed at night. Life is not easy when your husband is gone a lot of the time, but I cherish who he is and what God has called him to. I cannot imagine life without him, and I pray that all of you will remain faithful and wise so that you can know the beautiful fellowship that God can give you in a mate

Section Two

Personal Preparation (Chapters 10-19)

The discerning heart seeks knowledge. Proverbs 15:14 (NIV)

This section of the book is all about you! You will be asked some tough questions about yourself, and you may be a little discouraged at times, but that is fine. We need to do a complete inventory of ourselves before we make the big step into love and marriage. None of us are perfect. That is why Jesus died for us. We are all works in progress. The point is to be progressing.

The most important thing in relationships is not finding the right person. It is being the right person. God wants to develop character in you right now, and your character is the person that you are striving to be. Here are some probing thoughts to jumpstart your mind and heart towards personal preparation. Be careful, this might sting a little...

Are you growing in your relationship with Jesus Christ?
Are you the kind of person you would want to spend a lifetime with?
Do you constantly struggle with feelings of insecurity?
Are you obsessed with your weight, hair, face, clothes, or appearance?
Do you have difficulty finishing things after you start them?
Are you unreliable?
Are you constantly running late?
Do you always wait until the last minute?
Do you lose your cool easily?
Do you pout when you don't get what you want?
Are you jealous of other people's successes?
Do you compare yourself to others constantly?
Are you a messy person who never cleans up after yourself?
Were you spoiled growing up, and are you a spoiled brat still today?
Would you let your teenage child date someone just like you?
Do you look at pornography?
Do you have a serious problem with lust?
Do you lack discipline in prayer, the scriptures, and church attendance?
Are you sexually active?
Are there any addictions you struggle with?
Do you hop in and out of relationships?
Do you date just so you won't be the only person in your clique who doesn't?
Do you have a bad relationship with your parents? Why?
Do you lie a lot?
Can you be trusted on a date alone with someone's son or daughter?

Do you gossip?
Are you addicted to drama?
Do you blame others when it is your fault?

It is painful if you will answer these questions honestly, but it is necessary if you want to be the kind of person who is mature enough for a relationship. Don't worry. No one will grade you on this! You are the only one responsible for yourself, and no one will be looking over your shoulder or reading your mind as you tackle some of these issues. But please tell the truth to yourself. Don't take a shortcut and skim over these casually. Take the time to reflect on who you really are at this very moment. God is not surprised or offended. He already knows you better than you know yourself, and He loves you anyway!

This entire section will dig deeper into the real you and the person you want to be with questions just like these. God is transforming you into the image of His Son, Jesus Christ. That is good news. But it takes time and work, and I know you want to be the right person for your husband or wife. So here we go. Get ready to be challenged. Get ready to be changed!

The fear of the Lord teaches a man wisdom, and humility comes before honor. Proverbs 15:33 (NIV)

Chapter 10

17 Million Dollar Purity Plan

Therefore be careful how you walk, not as unwise men but as wise, making the most of your time, because the days are evil. So then do not be foolish, but understand what the will of the Lord is.
Ephesians 5:15-17 (NASB)

I should be a rich man. I've been doing some calculations, and here's what I've come up with: If I had back all the money I spent in high school on girlfriends and pseudo girlfriends, I'd be a millionaire. These expenses include, but are not limited to:

1. Stuffed animals on Valentine's Day
2. Relatively inexpensive but attractive jewelry for birthdays
3. Assorted Christmas presents
4. Flowers-just because I'm a sensitive sweet guy and sending flowers is what I was supposed to do so all the girl's friends would talk about how lucky she was
5. Three and a half month anniversary chocolates (you know you've celebrated silly anniversaries too, don't make fun of me!)
6. Dinner at Ruby Tuesday and tickets to a movie afterward (God for bid she wanted popcorn and a soda-that's another $75)
7. Doggone it, even the money for gas to drive to the movie theater which was 20 miles from my house!

I spent the bulk of the money I made from my part time jobs in high school on impressing girls, each of whom I just knew was "the one." If I had invested that money in a mutual fund that yielded a modest 13% return over the next thirty years, according to my math, it would roughly equal 17 million dollars. Oh, the high price of dating, the ridiculous cost of school age "love." I want my money back!

Ok, my 17 million dollar estimation is totally random and fictitious. No actual financial calculations were performed in the development of this illustration. But the point is valid: It costs money to date! The implied point is even more valid: It can cost a lot more than money to date the wrong person! In the next several chapters I'm going to labor to convince you of the benefits and pleasures of personal purity, as well as the risks and expenses of not yielding your passions and desires to Christ. I want to set the tone by helping you see that guarding your heart pays great dividends in every way imaginable.

Allow me to introduce the .00178% Rule. It states that approximately .00178% of middle school/high school/college dating relationships actually end in marriage. This is another entirely arbitrary, non scientific statistic, but reason with me. Think through all of your friends who have been in "serious" dating relationships. How many of them are still in those relationships? Quite a few, you say? Well then, what are the chances that the relationship will survive the years including college and post college, and end in wedded bliss? Take it from your good pal Steven: the chances are slim. From what I've witnessed in my admittedly short lifetime, the chances are about .00178%. Therefore, it is not wise to invest all of yourself in a relationship that will probably not last. It is-excuse my frankness-STUPID to give your heart away exclusively to a person who you'll probably break up with one day. It is dreadfully unproductive-even sinful-to pour all of your time, energy, emotions, hopes and dreams into a relationship that won't withstand the test of time, all the while missing opportunity after opportunity to know and glorify Christ in your youth.

If this sounds too harsh or unsympathetic to reality, perhaps you don't understand the concept of accountability. God has given you a life and allowed you to choose how you'll live it. You are building this life moment by moment, and your next moment isn't promised. Every breath you breathe is a gift from the Lord. Accountability means that since God gave you life and is, at this very moment, sustaining your life, you answer to Him for how you invest-or waste-the life He's given you. And you don't just answer to Him one day when you die, you answer to Him throughout your life, as you deal with the consequences of your decisions, good and bad. That's a tremendous responsibility! It's also an exciting possibility: God designed you, each and every part of you, on purpose. He calls you to do His will and then equips you through the Holy Spirit to do it.

What is the essence of the seventeen million dollar purity plan? It is that you stop wasting your life and devote yourself to the glory of God, no matter the cost. And no one is too young or too old to grasp and apply this, it begins today. Our key scripture, Ephesians. 5:16, couldn't be clearer: make the most of your time! Don't waste your life! Even if you can date tons of people throughout these formative years without becoming sexually active or going too far physically, there is a less obvious and equally deadly temptation to miss out. Maybe that sounds funny, that those who immerse themselves completely in relationship drama miss out...isn't that quite opposite the world's perspective?

According to current pop psychology, you must date various and sundry people before you find love and settle down. You should experiment sexually to see what suits your preferences and confirm compatibility. Love is a sort of game, and if you get tired of your teammate, hit the reset button and start over with someone else. And those who don't subscribe to this theory of love are supposedly "missing out." To me, missing out means staying up late at night arguing by telephone or Instant Messenger with someone you probably shouldn't be dating in the first place. Missing out means going to class every morning with the sole intention of impressing a certain guy, never experiencing the consuming joy of serving Christ with abandon. Missing out means a wasted life, comprised of time spent obsessing over appearance rather than character, pursuing popularity rather than favor with God.

Please note this crucially balancing disclaimer: there is a healthy way to conduct your love life. All forms of dating are not bad. It is not a sin to find a member of the opposite sex interesting and attractive. Further, it is not a sin to spend time getting to know that guy or girl better. And, if both interested parties are ready spiritually, physically, and emotionally, it's not a sin to date. But most of us end up with so much regret precisely because we are not ready. We are not yet established in our faith, with our eyes fixed on Jesus and our standards firmly rooted in Him. So we look for satisfaction in all the wrong places-or more frequently-all the wrong people. And it leaves us empty. And confounded. And, if you remember my opening illustration, broke!

I certainly wasted far too many hours building on faulty foundations which I thought were true love. I missed great opportunities to grow as a man of God, opting instead for the temporary pleasure and ultimate misery of flirting with, giving my heart away to, and often dating the wrong girls. Although I was a virgin on my wedding day, I compromised physically in ways that the world would say are no big deal, but to me, were only to be shared with my wife.

So allow the Lord to make you a truly rich young man or woman. As we journey through the next several chapters, I'll show you what kind of purity the Lord expects from you and how you can live it out. I'll show you how to avoid the distraction and destruction induced by false notions of love. A Christ-centered, grace empowered commitment to personal holiness and purity may not exactly bring you financial riches, but it will fill your heart with purpose, and leave you with no regret. True riches indeed!

Chapter 11

Girls Are Evil & Guys Are Dumb
(and other funny, incorrect assumptions)

Cliches abound concerning the two sexes. It seems like everyone has an analogy when it comes to the differences between guys and girls. Here are a few you may recognize.

Men are dogs, women are cats. Guys like to play and wrestle and get dirty and have fun. Just feed them and scratch their bellies and they will be happy. They are messy, but low maintenance. They are easy to figure out. Girls on the other hand are a bit more complex and involved. They may be moody. They are picky and neat, obsessed with being clean. You cannot always predict what they want, and they are full of surprises. They are high maintenance.

Men are waffles, women are spaghetti. Guys can compartmentalize everything, and like the squares on the top of a waffle, each one is able to hold syrup on its own. So guys take emotions and thoughts and put each one in its own little box without letting it touch or connect with any other emotion, feeling, or issue. Girls are like spaghetti. Each noodle is connected to and intertwined with every other noodle, and they are all inseparable. A woman's thoughts, feelings, and emotions are all connected to each other. They cannot pull one out by itself without all the others coming with it.

Men are from Mars, women are from Venus. Guys want to conquer and wage war, fight and show off their muscles and trophies. They want to destroy things! Girls want to be beautiful and mysterious, building a nest and nurturing children. They want to create things!

Do you see now why we just had to write a book on this? Though we will probably not have a single new, creative, earth-shattering revelation in these pages, we felt as if we just had to throw our two cents worth into such a colorful and vast issue as this one!

If you are a girl, I bet I can guess what you are thinking or have thought about boys at some point. Why do they act the way they do? Why are they so loud? Why are they so obnoxious? Why do they constantly show off? Why do they do crazy things that hurt their friends and themselves? Why do they constantly get into trouble? Why are they so mean to people sometimes? Why don't they dress nicer? Why don't they understand me? Why do they want to kill things and set things on fire?

Ladies, these are very good questions, and I am not even sure that you will understand once I explain it to you. I don't want to sound like a walking encyclopedia or come across too scientific, so I will keep it simple (plus I have some experience being a guy).

A man's greatest need is to be noticed and respected. This begins almost immediately after birth. When Jacob was less than a year old, we were at the doctor's office. He stood up on the table and began to beat the wall relentlessly while chanting something that sounded Stone Age. Dr. Hayek just laughed and told us that in all his years of pediatrics, all the little boys do that, but never had he seen a girl act in such a way. Boys have different chemicals and hormones than girls, and no matter now much our culture tries to blend the two sexes, we are vastly different and distinct. Men posture themselves and do things be noticed. When they are young and immature, they will pull a girl's pony tail or shoot a spit wad at the teacher. As the teen years approach, they will parade their developing muscles by cutting the sleeves off their t-shirts. Then it progresses to competitive sports or sports cars, big trucks, or a girlfriend. They do all these things to gain the recognition of their peers, male and female. Men build rapport by doing things and participating in activities together, like sports or fishing or cars. If you ask a guy what he did with his friends after a day with them, he can give you a play-by-play analysis. But try asking him what they talked about! He will be frightened by the question, and then he will simply respond with "Nothing."

And it continues throughout life. In college it is sports or girls or grades or fraternities. Then later it becomes a high-paying job, an expensive bass boat, or a large home. Maybe it is a deer head on the wall (or in my case a bear skin). Men want to be noticed and respected, so remember that ladies, the next time a guy says or does something weird that makes no sense to you!

Gentlemen, you have wondered some things about girls. Why do they talk so much? Why do they get so upset? Why do they cry so much? Why do they get their feelings hurt so easily? Why don't they ever just say what they feel? Why do they change their minds so much? Why do they think they are fat? Why do they love to shop so much? Why do they always give hints? What is so great about chocolate?

A woman's greatest need is to feel loved and secure. Women have an ability that men will never experience; they can give birth. God was really smart in doing this because men are sissies. If we had to give birth, the human race would cease to exist. We could not take the pain. Or maybe we could all just adopt.

Girls have a different chemical and physical make-up than guys and are not naturally as competitive and aggressive. Girls are more loving and nurturing, and I believe that is a natural instinct that God has given them as mothers. I saw it when Jacob was born. When we found out we were pregnant, my wife began the "nesting" process in our house. She wanted to create a safe and secure environment for her and the baby, so we remodeled and decorated his room with a farm and John Deere theme. We bought every baby-thing imaginable. She wanted him to be loved.

The reason why girls get more upset is not necessarily because they are more emotional, but because they are more likely to express what they feel than guys. The verbal part of a girl's brain is bigger than that of a guy, so the average woman says 25,000 words a day. The average man says 10,000 words a day. That is why girls talk so much! They have to. Women build rapport by giving report. They express how they feel, every last spaghetti noodle, and they tell secrets even when they are little girls. A guy may get confused when a woman is talking, because she jumps from one thing to another, and he thinks they have nothing to do with each other. But for her, they are totally connected. Remember, women don't put things in a box. It is all connected and when they talk it all sounds jumbled to a man but makes perfect sense to a woman.

So the man can tell that the woman is upset, and he asks the classic question, "Honey, what is wrong?" And as long as the grass is green and water is wet, she will respond by saying "Nothing." To the guy, that is insane. Of course something is wrong or she would not be pouting and crying. What she wants is for the man to talk, ask questions, probe deep into her heart and figure out what is wrong. Why? It shows her that he loves her and that he is willing to patiently deal with the issue. And she may honestly not know what is wrong! She just knows that she is upset, but she has to have time to sort out her feelings (noodles get sticky and messy). But if Charie asks me what is wrong, in classic man-fashion, I can access that file and tell her specifically what I am bothered by. I keep all my waffle squares separate. And I don't cry when I discuss it.

Women need order and organization because they want to feel safe and secure. That is why they clean and put so much effort into their appearance. Go to a house in a college town with four girls living there and it will be immaculate. You could eat off the floors. Go to a college house like that with four guys, and the floor could eat you. Girls take more time getting ready than guys because the small details are important. The guy just wants to go eat, but the girl wants to look pretty (even though some guys think girls make them wait just to prove that girls truly rule the universe).

So the stereotypes, even though they are shallow, have reasons for existing. Guys call girls evil because some girls can be hurtful, unforgiving, jealous and vindictive if they are hurt or if they don't get what they want. But that is not all girls. And girls call guys dumb, because, well, sometimes we are. And other times we just don't know how to express how we really feel in words. (We grunt). Don't forget that girls mature sooner than guys emotionally, and it takes a few years for guys to catch up. So we are not really dumb, we're just not where you need us to be, yet. But we are on our way, baby!

So what do girls need? A guy that listens and tries to understand. A guy who is thoughtful and considerate. A guy who can talk about how he feels. A guy who is wholeheartedly into her and her alone.

What do guys need? A girl who will go places and do things with him. A girl who lets him play and have friends of his own. A girl who respects him and tells him so. A girl who brags on him and tells him he is the best.

Pointers for Guys (Especially Husbands)

1. Don't talk too much. Shut up and listen to the female!
2. Buy her things when she is not with you (this means you were thinking about her).
3. Call her often and call when you say you will call. Never be late for anything.
4. Don't flirt with other girls or even look at them EVER.
5. Take her out- girls love to get dressed up for a classy date now and then.
6. Write her notes often, and if you are the man, write her poetry

Pointers for Girls (Especially Wives)

1. Give him space- don't crowd him, let him have friends and do things with them.
2. Brag on him - his grades, sports, anything you can think of as an encouragement.
3. Speak well of him in front of other people, he will feel like the King of the world.
4. Show interest in his hobbies (if possible) and go places with him that he likes.
5. Be patient when he is emotionally or verbally constipated - don't give up!
6. Cook for him or bring him food, just trust me on this one. It works.

Chapter 12
Who Lied To You?

So Jesus was saying to those Jews who had believed Him, "If you continue in My word, then you are truly disciples of Mine; and you will know the truth, and the truth will make you free."
John 8:31-32 (NASB)

I hate being lied to. I am a very honest person, and I expect honesty from the people in my life. In fact, one of my favorite things about God is His trustworthiness. He never exaggerates or stretches the truth, and He never misleads His children, He is the God of complete truth. However, the world has been filling our heads with lies about our sexuality and desires for love since the day our sensory perceptions were operable. Lies spill forth from our television screens, our computer monitors, the speakers of our radios, the pages of our newspapers...lies, lies, lies...everywhere! Personally, I've had just about enough of it. In this chapter, I want to confront a few of the most crippling lies that many of us believe about relationships and combat them with the truth of God's Word. According to our key verse, John 8:32, we can only be free when we know the truth.

First of all, I want you to understand where the lies come from. Ultimately, all lies come from Satan. Jesus was speaking to a group of antagonists one day, and he broke it down like this:

You are of your father the devil, and you want to do the desires of your father. He was a murderer from the beginning, and does not stand in the truth because there is no truth in him. Whenever he speaks a lie, he speaks from his own nature, for he is a liar and the father of lies.
John 8:44 (NASB)

Did you see that? Satan is the father of lies. All lies originate with him. When you have a thought that is contrary to the will of God, it is a thought from Satan. Ladies, when you see Britney Spears parading her half-naked, emaciated body across the set of her latest video, it initiates the lie that you should look like her. The media is presenting you with their idea of true sexuality, when in fact, nothing could be further from the truth. Satan is lying to you through the media. Do you see how this works in such a subtle way? Guys, you are lying to yourself when you know you are going too far physically with a young lady, and you justify it by thinking "I'll stop if she tells me to stop. After all, that's her responsibility." True young men of God recognize such cowardly excuses as lies of the enemy and reject them, overcoming them with the truth of God.

Now that we've pinpointed where lies come from, let's get specific about some of the lies we believe about relationships. I've chosen to focus primarily on lies that cause us to panic about the lack of relationship, as Clayton will focus more on the temptations of the relationship itself in later chapters. As we evaluate these lies, our eyes will be opened to the truth of God's Word, which is able to set us free.

Lie #1: Everybody else has someone but me.

I attended a very small Christian college where I spent four wonderful years learning, growing, and developing as a man of God. I also happened to meet my wife our freshman year, which makes me forever grateful to North Greenville College. I wasn't the only young hopeful who graduated from North Greenville engaged to be married. In fact, it seemed that on the NGC campus, love bloomed and blossomed out of control, in season and out. When the weather got warm around April, the courtyards became littered with starry-eyed couples. And oh, how the diamond engagement rings did abound! In fact, many of us jokingly developed an unofficial slogan to reflect the astounding volume of marriage proposals which seemed to take place each year: North Greenville College; A ring by Spring or your money back!

A lot of single students were quite discouraged (and sometimes disgusted!) by the lovey, cuddly, gushy Spring marriage fever festivities. When everybody around you seems to be in love, it's easy to feel left out. Maybe you've felt that way before. Maybe you feel that way currently. The lie goes like this: everyone else is happily in love except you. You'll never find anyone. Something must be wrong with you...This lie can get down deep inside of you and destroy your capacity for contentment in Christ. If you believe this lie, you'll soon find it impossible to wait for the Lord to fulfill your romantic ambitions. And you'll hurry to scratch your emotional itches, compromising your integrity and negotiating your standards along the way.

God's Truth: You're not the only one, and even if you were, Jesus is enough.

When I present seminars on love, dating and purity I always ask for a show of hands to see how many of the students are presently in exclusive dating relationships. I've performed this experiment with middle school, high school and college students more times than I can count, and the results may surprise you. On average, only five to ten percent of the students indicate that they're in a relationship. And I guarantee you that only five to ten percent of that group are genuinely happy and fulfilled in the relationship. So don't believe the lie! The truth is, you're not alone. And when you consider the real presence of Jesus Christ in your life, and His sufficiency to give you the desires of your heart in His perfect time, you're most certainly not alone!

Lie #2: God is mad at me for my desires.
God's Truth: God put the desire there!

In his book Knowledge of the Holy, A.W. Tozer asserts that what comes to your mind when you think about God is the most important thing about you. I agree. Nowhere is this more applicable than in our perspective on love and dating. If you think God is angry at you for being attracted to the opposite sex, you've missed it. If you visualize your heavenly Father shaking his head in utter disappointment every time you dream of your wedding day, you've been lied to. Not only is God not aggravated and angered by these desires, he put the desires there!

Guys, remember the first time you had that weird feeling in the pit of your stomach about a girl? It's the feeling that instantly transforms you into a blundering idiot every time she walks into the room. It's the magical force that causes you to say and do dumb things at the very moment you so desperately need to be suave and impressive. That feeling, that force, that mystical, intangible desire in your gut was put there by God. He designed you to desire a significant other. Think back to the Garden of Eden. Adam was sinless, healthy, and in right relationship with God, but strangely incomplete. Genesis 2:18 records the conclusion to the dilemma: Then the LORD God said, "It is not good for the man to be alone; I will make him a helper suitable for him." There it is, write it down and put it on your wall: It is not good for man to be alone. God gave you the desire for a relationship without regret. It is a reflection of the innate desire each human has for God.

Lie #3: God can't or won't fulfill my desires
God's truth: He "is able to do far more abundantly beyond all that we ask or think, according to the power that works within us" Ephesians 3:20 (NASB)

This lie is sneaky. Most of us would never say God can't fulfill our desires. If we were sitting together eating a hamburger and I asked you, "Do you believe God can do anything?" you would most certainly answer with a resounding "Of course!" However, I'm learning that our vocalizations about what we believe are only validated by corresponding actions that proclaim the same belief. Put simply, when you run around dating people like you're trying on shoes, your actions suggest that you don't believe God can do anything. If you believed that, you'd focus your attention and energies on serving Him wholeheartedly. Frantic drama and incessant worrying about true love have no place in the life of a Christ follower. Devote yourself to being the right person instead of finding the right person.

Others of us believe God can bring us love that lasts a lifetime, but sometimes it seems He refuses to do so. If you're one of the many would-be lovers waiting on your time in the sun, wondering if God's forgotten about you, let me present you with a few reasons why you may still be waiting.

1. You're not ready. This isn't always the case, and if God waited until we were perfect to bring us someone to marry, weddings would only take place in heaven. However, in the final section of this book, we'll present red flags that may need to be dealt with in your life before you're ready for the pains and strains of love.

2. He wants you single for a reason right now. This thought has certainly been explained and exploited a great deal, but it's worth mentioning again. Your single years are very valuable. Forgive me if I sound parental, but you really do have much more free time in your singleness than you'll have when you're married. So if God wants you single during these years, consider it a privilege. He has special assignments for you during this season, and He'll hook you up when the time is right!

3. When all other logic fails, remember that God is God. He loves you, and He knows what He's doing. Sometimes that powerful truth is all that can transcend our uneasiness about the future.

There are many more lies we believe, and endless variations of these basic deceptions can hold us captive. Deception is powerful precisely because you don't know you're being deceived. If you knew, you wouldn't fall for it. May today be the day that these seductive lies are exposed and rendered ineffective in your life. "Then you will know the truth, and the truth will make you free."

Chapter 13

Flee And Follow

Therefore, if anyone cleanses himself from these things, he will be a vessel for honor, sanctified, useful to the Master, prepared for every good work. Now flee from youthful lusts and pursue righteousness, faith, love and peace, with those who call on the Lord from a pure heart. 2 Timothy 2:21-22 (NASB)

Why are the attendees of the average youth group just as sexually promiscuous as their un-churched peers? Why is there often very little distinction in dress, speech and sexual disposition between teenagers who profess Christ as Savior and those who don't? I'm constantly searching for answers to these questions as I travel through the country in ministry. I'm saddened that we, as ministers of the gospel, have often done such a poor job in equipping students to be pure and holy. It's disheartening to see the fruit of this lack of equipment displayed in the lives of students. What are we doing wrong? Why are so few young people making it to the altar of marriage with their purity intact, while so many others are stopping far short of God's standard for relationships without regret?

Partially to blame is our emphasis on entertainment rather than exposition of the Bible in youth ministry. Another culprit is this sex drenched culture that students have to wade through in the quest for long term purity in this generation.

However, a less obvious source of our ineffective discipleship is our weak and one sided explanations of what living for God looks like. There are two broad practical components involved in the battle against lust and relational drama. When faced with temptation, you must flee the sin, and then you must follow Christ wholeheartedly. The problem is, we've often done a poor job of motivating you to flee the sinful things, and we've given you even poorer instruction for how to do so. And even when we powerfully explain the gravity of sin and beg you to flee it, we frequently stop right there. So we end up with students who are running scared but have nothing to pursue. And soon, you get tired of running and give up. No wonder we're in such a mess.

Let's turn to scripture to get it right. Our key verse for this chapter describes the kind of person that I believe you are longing to be, a vessel for honor, sanctified, useful to the Master, prepared for every good work. One of the greatest motivations for staying pure is to understand that God has terrific things planned for your life. He wants to use you to bring Him glory. But He can't use you according to your maximum potential unless you flee your youthful lusts. Let's talk about those lusts for a moment. I believe the lust is different for guys and girls (more on this in a later chapter), but the basic idea here is to get away from them. To flee them. To run for your life. Get out of town. Get the picture? What should you do? You should flee. What should you flee? Lusts. What kind of lusts? Youthful ones. I find it interesting that Paul, writing to Timothy, who was a young man, specifically warned against youthful lusts. Our lusts in the area of relationships are never stronger than they are in our youthful years.

Honestly, as Clayton has often said, from the age of twelve to twenty-two you don't have hormones...you are a hormone! And physically your body is changing so quickly during these years that you often don't know what to do about all the physical temptations that surge through your body or the emotional roller-coaster of your desires for companionship. When a guy sees a girl and thinks she's pretty, that's a good, healthy, normal reaction. When he begins to let his mind run wild with sexual thoughts about her body, staring at her and drooling all over himself, the desire has gone entirely wrong. It has become perverted, and now it is lust. When a young lady dreams of her wedding day and someone to love her and call her sugar, baby, honey, sweetheart or whatever sappy gushy nickname she prefers, that's a good desire. But when that desire overwhelms her desire to know God in a deep and real way it becomes a distraction in her life. It is now lust, and it can ruin her spiritual future.

So Paul says "flee youthful lusts." Run, Forest! I know the lusts are strong. In fact they are stronger than you. You cannot beat them. You must run from them. They will destroy you. Flee! As fast as you can! What does that mean? It means to get as far away as possible at an accelerated pace. I will elaborate on how to grapple with temptation and win (or at least learn from your defeat) in a later chapter.

Lest this chapter becomes one sided and wade only in the necessary, but shallow waters of "what not to do," let's look at the second half of the command-the command to follow. Paul instructs Timothy to follow after righteousness, faith, love and peace. Those are certainly virtues worth pursuing, but ultimately, it's Jesus Himself-not His principles, but His person-that you should pursue. And since the word follow doesn't quite convey the proper power, I suggest that the call to purity is ultimately a call to a holy obsession with Christ.

The kind of obsession I'm advocating is not obsession with religious rules and regulations. Jesus said in Matthew 22:37-38 "You shall love the LORD your God will all your heart, and with all your soul and with all your mind. This is the great and foremost commandment." Jesus meant to imply that all of life revolves around the fundamental premise of loving God. Your love isn't devoted to an impersonal force who is administrating the universe without any direct involvement. The Lord is your God-it's personal! What contentment this truth inspires! What security it assures! You are not to be obsessed with Christian checklists, or with moral living. You are to be obsessed with a personal God...your God, who is the powerful Maker of heaven and earth.

Now here's the obsessive part. You are to love him with all your heart, soul and mind. That leaves nothing out. Please understand, you don't have the option of committing selected portions of yourself to the Lord, this is a full fledged obsession. That's what it means to follow. Usually, when a young man commits himself wholeheartedly to an athletic endeavor, people applaud his discipline, toughness and talent. Similarly, when a young lady gives all of herself to studying hard and keeping her eyes on future academic goals, she is hailed as a responsible and focused individual with a deep understanding of proper priorities. When an adult harnesses all of his mental, emotional, and physical capabilities in order to make lots of money, that person is venerated as a savvy businessman with great ambition. Nothing is wrong with athletics, academics, or financial success. But why is it okay in our society to be obsessed with everything but the God of the universe?

Most of your friends will never understand what drives you to be radically obsessed with God. They will assure you that you're missing out, that you're going overboard, and that you're taking Christianity too far. Too far? Is all of your heart, all of your soul, and all of your mind too far? According to Jesus, it's the least you can offer to God. Anything else that you become obsessed with will fade away. Obsession with popularity is an empty obsession because popularity comes and goes. Most of the friends you have now will graduate, move on, and forget about you. Obsession with material things is hollow because things become worn out and obsolete. Obsession with romantic relationships is disappointing because even the best relationship is imperfect. Obsession with the person of Jesus Christ is exhilarating and ultimately satisfying because the obsession of His glory is the reason you were made. Is any other obsession really worth it? Is there anything else worth living for?

When you become truly obsessed with Jesus, a lot of the other stuff in life begins to seem pretty small and insignificant. That's why Jesus demands that we "seek first the Kingdom of God and His righteousness" and promises that "all these things will be added." (Matthew 6:33) He knows how to fill your desires. He knows how to make your dreams come true. Throw all of yourself into knowing Him and making Him known. Let your friends laugh and call you a fool. Let them accuse you of taking your faith too seriously. And let them see the glory of God fill your life as He provides your every need and becomes your true satisfaction.

Chapter 14
Walk, Stand , Sit

How blessed is the man who does not walk in the counsel of the wicked, Nor stand in the path of sinners, Nor sit in the seat of scoffers! But his delight is in the law of the LORD, And in His law he meditates day and night. Psalms 1:1-2 (NASB)

We rarely fall into sin. We don't ever fall away from God. The word fall indicates an abrupt, unpreventible accident which is out of our control. That's not a very accurate description of what happens when we sin against God. To make this practical and meaningful, I want you to think of a recent sin that you committed. It doesn't have to be a "big" sin, just something in your life that you did that was not pleasing to God. Did you really fall into that sin? Or did you decide to do it, possibly by making bad choices that led up to it? Were there several warning signs that what you were doing wasn't right, such as a guilty conscience or a scripture verse that popped into your mind?

For the purpose of a common illustration, let's use the obvious examples of sexual sin, lust, or preoccupation with romance. If you've recently sinned in these areas (and there's a good chance you have) I'm guessing that there were several events and thoughts surrounding that sin. First of all, you knew it was wrong. Sometimes we can justify sin in our minds, but in our hearts, those of us who have the Holy Spirit living in us know when we're out of line. This conviction from the Holy Spirit is meant to prevent us from sinning against God and to draw us back to Him when we do fall short. Secondly, you probably put yourself in a situation which made it easier to mess up, thereby making it difficult to stay pure. Thirdly, you chose to gratify the desires of your flesh rather than the desires of Jesus. Do you see that this can hardly be described as falling into sin? It is a subtle process of deception that slowly, but surely, works its way into our everyday lives.

Therefore, it is more Biblical to say that we progress into sin. Our key passage indicates this progression. In Psalm 1, David describes two types of men, the one who pleases God and the one who does not. In the very first verse David demonstrates how slippery the progression of sin can be. In describing the person who pleases God, David recognizes a careful avoidance of the things that lead up to sin: he does not walk in the counsel of the wicked, nor stand in the path of sinners, nor sit in the seat of scoffers. See the progression of sin? First we walk near it, then we stand around it, and eventually we sit down in it! I've seen this happen countless times in my life. During my high school years, I would often have a negative attitude about something my parents said or something they asked me to do. By allowing this attitude to pass through my mind, I was walking near the sin of dishonoring my mother and father. However, by dwelling on the attitude and letting it simmer in my mind, I was standing around it. And finally, by saying something disrespectful to them or rolling my eyes, I was sitting down in the sin, which produced great tension and grief. It all started with an attitude, which I should have recognized and surrendered to the Lordship of Christ. Walk, stand, sit...a predictable but powerful progression. I observe this pattern time after time in my interaction with Holly. Here's a fictitious example in the form of a script: Ok, it's not entirely fictitious, but minor details have been altered to protect the guilty (me!) and make it a little funnier.

Holly: Can you clean the showers for me sometime today?
Steven: (not out loud) What? Didn't I just clean them?
   ***Note from the author: For a male who is just entering the world of marriage, cleaning the showers once a week seems overboard, almost obsessive. This most probably stems from the habits I developed in the college dorm, where we cleaned the showers-I'm embarrassed to say-once a semester-maybe. Now back to the script.
Steven: (out loud) Sure, I guess.
Holly: Thanks.
Steven: (not out loud) Why does she have to be so finicky about the showers? They're clean enough! They're not caked in mud or anything. There are no bugs crawling around. They'll just get dirty again...I hate cleaning the showers!
Steven: Stupid showers....
Holly: What?
Steven: I just cleaned them. I get tired of....

Now the complaining starts. And I'm sinning by being a bratty and whiny husband. Did you see my attitude slowly going downhill? It started with negative thoughts, which I could have overcome with truth: No big deal, I'll clean 'em. It'll only take ten minutes. But I let it progress. Walk, stand, sit. Negative attitude=walking, dwelling on the wrong attitude=standing, complaining and disrespecting my wife=sitting.

Maybe you can't relate to that example. Here's one a little closer to home. I gave my life to Christ when I was a sixteen year old junior in high school. About three months after my conversion, a young lady started to show a lot of romantic interest in me. She was a pretty girl, fun to talk to, athletic, smart...what would be wrong with dating her? What could it hurt? Well, it so happened that although this girl professed Christ as her Savior, she wasn't pursuing Christ with all of her heart, and I was. In my heart, I knew that dating her would drag me down spiritually, but I ignored this reality and dated her anyway. No harm done so far-no big sin, no big problem. I even justified it in my mind: "I can help her grow spiritually!" (This may be the biggest self-deception in the book.) But I was walking in a dangerous place by dating someone who didn't have the same spiritual passion and priorities that I did. We dated a few months, the relationship progressed, and late one night we made out for the first time in the basement of her parents' house. I knew this was going to lead to worse things and that it was sending my mind racing in places it had no business dwelling. I was standing where I should not have stood, all the while making excuses as to why it was okay. And the physical experimentation boundaries kept getting pushed further and further away from God's standards of purity the longer we stayed in the relationship. Thank God that we finally broke up before the sin progressed to the point of sexual intercourse. But I lost a lot of focus and missed a lot of spiritual growth opportunities because of the slippery, subtle progression of sin in my life.

Isn't it clear? Can't you see how it happens? Walk, stand, sit. Thought, action, habit. It's easy to see this progression but difficult to guard against it. In fact, even David, who explained this pattern of sin for us in Psalm 1, who was the greatest king in the history of the nation of Israel, and who was a man after God's own heart, fell prey to this terrible progression in the later years of his life and experienced first hand its cruel repercussions.

The familiar account is recorded in 2 Sameul 11:1-4:
Then it happened in the spring, at the time when kings go out to battle, that David sent Joab and his servants with him and all Israel, and they destroyed the sons of Ammon and besieged Rabbah. But David stayed at Jerusalem. Now when evening came David arose from his bed and walked around on the roof of the king's house, and from the roof he saw a woman bathing; and the woman was very beautiful in appearance. So David sent and inquired about the woman. And one said, "Is this not Bathsheba, the daughter of Eliam, the wife of Uriah the Hittite?" David sent messengers and took her, and when she came to him, he lay with her; and when she had purified herself from her uncleanness, she returned to her house.

David paid a high price for his sexual sin. In an attempt to cover this sin David had Bathsheba's husband, Urriah the Hittite, killed on the front lines of battle. The baby born to Bathsheba died as an infant, and no amount of repentance could spare the child's life. The consequences of this sin reverberated throughout the generations of David's descendants and was an unquenchable source of contention in his family and personal life for the years to come. It is tragically ironic that the patron saint who so firmly grasped the dreadful progression of sin was taken captive and destroyed by its allures. A brief study of the account reveals just how exactly the sin was a textbook example of walking, standing, and sitting in sexual sin. David was walking around his roof at the time when the kings go out to battle. David was the king of Israel, and should have been leading his men into battle, but he stayed home and walked around the roof of his palace. It is very important to note that if David would have been where he should have been, this sin wouldn't have occurred. It is the same for you. If you don't date the wrong people, flip through the wrong channels, and hang out in the wrong chatrooms, you'll have a much greater chance of not doing the wrong thing. Don't walk where you don't want to camp out. Don't camp out where you don't want to live.

As David was walking, he noticed Bathsheba. By this point, David is in great trouble. He is now standing and contemplating taking another man's wife. When you find yourself standing on the brink of sexual sin, do not stand and contemplate. Do not justify the sin in your mind or fill your head with excuses. Begin to fight the lies immediately with the truth of God's Word. If David would have come to his senses at this point and reminded himself of the goodness of God and his responsibility as God's appointed leader of a nation, perhaps things would have ended differently. But he didn't. And things ended badly. He not only sat, he laid with her, and his life was never the same. God forgave David and still loved him, but the damage was done, and David would never fully recover.

Sin is slippery. We don't usually wake up one day and decide to ruin our testimony. We progress into it. Are you slipping right now? Are you creating opportunity for sin to ruin your life? Are you ignoring God's warning signs? Evaluate yourself honestly, and do not walk, stand or sit anywhere near the evils of sexual immorality. The price is too high.

Chapter 15

I Wanna Be A Tree

He will be like a tree firmly planted by streams of water,
Which yields its fruit in its season
And its leaf does not wither;
And in whatever he does, he prospers. Psalms 1:3 (NASB)

I've shared some dumb sermon illustrations over the years, but one stands out as the dumbest. It's called the grand finale illustration, and I've shared it in more churches and college meetings than I care to remember. I wish I could take it back. The least I can do is make fun of it now.

The illustration describes three different types of fireworks. Since I worked in a firework stand as a young boy every July and December for seven years, I'm an expert on the subject. The three types of fireworks, broadly speaking, are duds, pretty neats, and grand finales. This illustration compared the Christian lives of the listeners to the different types of fireworks.

It went something like this:

(Loud, dramatic preacher voice) "Some of you are 'duds' in your walk with God. Your outside packaging looks nice, but there's no fire; your witness to this world is one big disappointment. You just make a little noise, fizzle, and sputter, but there's no explosion. You're a dud!

Others of you are 'pretty neat' Christians. Most fireworks make pretty colors, loud noises, and when they're done, everyone says 'That was pretty neat.' But it's just average, there's nothing memorable about a 'pretty neat' firework. And some of you are just average in your walk with God.

But let me tell you the kind of Christian I want to be: I want to be a grand finale for Jesus. The grand finale is the one they save for last. It's the one that gets everybody's attention. It's spectacular to watch. It's loud, and bright, and unforgettable. That's what God wants you to be...a grand finale, lighting up this dark world..."

And on and on I'd go, saying something that wasn't really true. God doesn't want me to be a grand finale, or any kind of firework for that matter, because all fireworks have one thing in common: they burn up and burn out! No matter how pretty the colors or glorious the noises, the grand finale eventually comes to an end. Some analogy, huh? Forgive me please.

That's not the kind of purity we want to advocate in this book. Grand finale purity means you make a commitment to be pure, and reaffirm that commitment each time you hear a moving sermon or an inspirational song. But grand finale Christianity, with its short term and external focus, will not enable you to stay pure in a consistent, lifelong way. So I've developed a new illustration, a better one. It's based on our key scripture, Psalm 1:3. I don't want to be a grand finale anymore. I want to be A TREE!

Nothing very exciting about that. No sound effects to go along with that illustration. A tree isn't very explosive or dynamic. But it's stable. And steady. And lasting. And that's what I want for my life, and for your life. Deep roots. A firm foundation. A tree. Actually, the more I think about it, the more exciting this aspiration to treedom becomes. Psalm 1 says that if I am like a tree I will be firmly planted by streams of water, I will yield my fruit in season, my leaf will not wither and in whatever I do, I will prosper. Not bad!

What is the tree's job? To stay planted by the streams of water and to grow. Long term purity is not something you can manufacture with a once-a-year commitment; it must be nurtured by daily communion with God. And long term purity is not a shallow, surface level checklist. It is a deep, abiding, rooted relationship with Christ that will display itself in a pure heart and pure actions.

It's very difficult to have a long-term perspective on life and purity in our very short term culture. We are told to satisfy our desires right now with very little regard for the future. Sexual purity is called inhibition and sexual sin is called liberation. However, when you understand long term purity from God's perspective, the exact opposite is true. To be pure before God is true liberty; anything else is bondage. It's hard to understand this in our youth, when our hormones are raging, and marriage seems miles away. It's nearly impossible to want to be a tree- a plain, boring, simple tree- in the American frenzy of sexuality, appearance worship, and messed up definitions of love. But in the long term it's the strong and steady Christians with deep roots who are blessed, happy, and to be envied.

When I was a junior in high school I was hanging out with several of my "friends" (people who treat you the way I'm about to report being treated are not friends) one Friday evening before a local football game. They were all a few years older than me, and several of them were drinking; a few others were smoking weed. Since I was the youngest one in the crowd, and I was one of the only ones not drinking or getting high, I felt pretty uncomfortable. For some reason, one of the guys in the group decided to pick on me and get a few laughs at my expense. "Furtick," he began, "have you ever been with a woman?" I knew where the conversation was going, that he was going to brag about his sexual exploits and make fun of me for my sexual inexperience, so I braced myself and answered honestly, "Naw, man, I've never slept with a girl." I said it with a trace of shame and embarrassment. I scanned the faces of the other guys sitting around, and they all wore proud smirks as if to say "What a loser." The guy who had initiated the conversation to begin with laughed at me and responded, "You're a lost little boy." The whole group laughed and nodded in agreement. "Any guy your age," the instigator continued, "who hasn't gotten any yet, is a little boy. A pitiful little boy..." He went on tearing me apart for what seemed like hours. I sat with my head drooped, speechless and defenseless, humiliated, and waited for it to end. My emotions were overwhelming, a combination of feeling angry, helpless and stupid. I was the only professing virgin in the room, and I was being crucified for it.

Fast forward ten years. I'm now married, happy, and secure in Christ. My wife is beautiful, my ministry is fruitful, and my life, all around, couldn't be better. I often wish I could run into the young man who made a public spectacle of me that Friday night so long ago. I wish I could show him a picture of my incredible wife and tell him about my wedding day. Because on my wedding day, Holly looked me in the eye, and she didn't tell me I was a loser because I was a virgin. She didn't tell me I was a lost little boy because I'd never had sex. She told me I was a real man. And she thanked me for waiting on her.

Please understand that long-term purity has short-term consequences that aren't always pleasant. People will laugh at you and mock you. People may reject you and refuse to include you in their little groups, or invite you to their parties. And it will hurt. But Psalm 1:3 says that you will be like a tree, firmly planted by the water of the Word and Sprit of God. He will comfort you and affirm you on the hard days when it seems that you're the only one staying pure. He will deepen your faith in Him and see to it that you yield your fruit in season. He'll bring you real love, at the right time, with the right person. He'll insure that your leaf does not whither. Sexual sin is fun for a season. It's fun to brag about, and it's thrilling to experience. But the thrill quickly fades, and the things you used to brag about begin to feel shameful. When you do it right, you have no regret. You are planted. Your future rests squarely in the capable hands of God. I don't know about you, but I don't want to burn out. I don't want to live for right now, with no regard for the future. I want to be a tree!

Chapter 16
Hate It, Starve It, Outsmart It

...so that no advantage would be taken of us by Satan, for we are not ignorant of his schemes. 2 Corinthians 2:11 (NASB)

I can spot it a mile away. It's the look of shame. The look of trepidation. The look of "I can't believe I'm about to tell you this." It's the look on the face of a young man who has just approached me to discuss the forbidden subject...LUST. They line up to confide in me after I preach on the subject of purity, and their struggles and stories are all too familiar. "I'm trying to pray and read my Bible, I'm going to church and all the youth group meetings, and I just can't stop lusting. It's killing me spiritually." I see relief spread across their faces when I explain that they're not weird, and that not only are they not the only guys who have struggled with lust, but it is a sin that I have personally struggled with. In fact, would it surprise you to learn that nine out of ten Christian guys identify lust as the number one sin that keeps them from a vibrant relationship with God? (That statistic is road tested, I've unofficially surveyed thousands of young men and the results are astounding) Admittedly, the problem of sexual lust is primarily a male struggle, but it's certainly familiar territory for females as well. I won't revisit Clayton's discussion on the differences between guys and gals, I'll just say that the following principles apply to all of us, male and female alike.

Since I've had so many conversations with students concerning lust, and since it's been a recurring struggle in my own life, I've spent an enormous amount of time developing Christ centered and practical strategies dealing with this debilitating sin. The following three steps for dealing with lust are not magical formulas. They are not exhaustive plans for defeating lust in your life. I don't want to set you up to believe that I've finally unlocked the secret weapon against lust, and I'm about to unleash it into your life so that you'll never have to lose another battle against lust. The disease of lust can't be cured by a list, and it can't really be fully explored in a single chapter. There are several excellent resources which are entirely devoted to this specific struggle, such as Every Man's Battle by Stephen Arterburn and Fred Stoeker, and Not Even a Hint by Joshua Harris. However, I want to spend a few moments writing to you as if we were having a face to face, one on one conversation about your struggle with lust. I want to share from my heart some strategies that will help you to wage and win this crucial battle.

To defeat any sin, you must first hate it. You must see the sin like God sees it. The greatest reason we hate our sin is that God is holy, and sin separates us from Him. Sin is an assault against the very nature and person of God. Sin nailed Jesus to the cross and made His suffering necessary. So we must hate sin. Specifically, we must hate our sin. It's easy for us to hate the sins of others, particularly the sins of Hollywood, abortion doctors, and crooked political figures. But look in your own heart and acknowledge the sin that keeps you from the abundant life God promised. John 10:10 says that the thief only comes to steal, kill, and destroy. When Satan perverts your God-given desires for love and sexuality, he is stealing from you. Your unconfessed sin is killing you spiritually. And lust will ultimately destroy you, along with all of the plans God has designed for your life. That's why you must hate it. I often tell students to get a "Holy Ghost attitude" with the sin of lust. It has been holding you down long enough. It has kept you from a white hot relationship with God long enough. When will you get sick of it? When will you realize that it only feels good momentarily, then it dumps you off and leaves you for dead? Hate your lust, or you'll never defeat it.

However, hating sin isn't enough to beat it. You must learn to starve it. This means to cut it off at the root. It means to unplug it at the source. Often we do the exact opposite. We feed, nourish, and cultivate our lusts for pleasure and love. If you have unmonitored access to the internet, and pornography or inappropriate chat room behavior is a struggle for you, what in the world are you thinking? It isn't enough to pray that God would deliver you from these temptations, you need to start starving the sin by eliminating as many opportunities to fail as possible. Maybe you should have your parents or roommate put a password on the computer and limit your time on the internet to times when they're in the room keeping you accountable. If that doesn't work, I've got a brilliant solution: cancel your internet subscription! Or throw the blasted computer out the window! Whatever it takes, you must starve your sin. If you really hate it, you will starve it. If you'll starve it, you'll gradually experience victory and freedom.

If you think this is too drastic, consider the words of Jesus:
You have heard that it was said, "YOU SHALL NOT COMMIT ADULTERY"; but I say to you that everyone who looks at a woman with lust for her has already committed adultery with her in his heart. If your right eye makes you stumble, tear it out and throw it from you; for it is better for you to lose one of the parts of your body, than for your whole body to be thrown into hell. If your right hand makes you stumble, cut it off and throw it from you; for it is better for you to lose one of the parts of your body, than for your whole body to go into hell. Matthew 5:27-30 (NASB)

How appropriate that the context of this bizarre command revolves around the subject of sexual lust! And Jesus doesn't advise you to do anything extreme like get rid of your computer, or to confess your struggle with lust, masturbation or pornography to another mature believer so that you will be held accountable. He would never get that drastic would He? Actually, He goes many steps further. He says you'd be better off tearing out your right eye or hacking off your right hand and throwing it away than allowing the cancer of lust to dominate your heart. Has Jesus lost His mind? He's not advocating self-mutilation by any stretch of the imagination, as this would directly contradict other commands in scripture. He is simply expressing that no measure is too great to ensure your sexual purity. Be pure, by any means necessary. Whatever it takes, guard your heart (Proverbs 4:23). Be holy, regardless of the cost.

Holly and I recently started getting Victoria Secret catalogues, replete with seductive, sleazy models, in our mailbox. I generally check the mail at our house, and the first time one of these catalogues showed up, I thought it was a mistake. I checked the name of the addressee, and to make matters worse, it was MY name on the mailing label. Holly had ordered something by phone from this company using my credit card, they locked us into their mailing list, and now Victoria's Secret catalogues were being sent to the Reverend Steven Furtick! I was horrified. I corresponded with them and requested to be taken off the mailing list. It didn't work, and the catalogues began to flood the Furtick household! At least one comes every two weeks. Although I love my wife deeply and consider her to be the most attractive person in the world, these catalogues recently became a temptation for me.

One day I even began to scan through one, justifying it by thinking "Well, I need to see exactly how filthy this stuff is..." You know, if you give yourself long enough, you can justify just about anything. So I decided to starve, unplug, and cut off this temptation. You may think this is a little psycho, but instead of simply throwing it away where I could possibly get it out of the trash can later, I rolled it up and stuck it in the toilet. I let it sit for a moment, then I took it out and shoved it to the bottom of the bathroom garbage pail, so that if I was tempted to look at it later, it would be covered in toilet water at the bottom of the nasty bathroom waste receptacle. That's not being psycho, it's getting serious! Starve your sin. Ladies, if you find yourself being tempted by some silver tongued guy who tells you everything you want to hear, don't get alone with him. If certain magazines and TV shows cause you to lust or feel discontent with the way you look, quit putting that stuff in your mind. Your purity is worth it!

Finally, you must begin to outsmart the sin that has ensnared you. This may sound odd, and you may be wondering exactly what I mean. It's actually simple, and it is the most helpful piece of advice I've ever shared regarding recurring sins like lust. In our key verse, 2 Corinthians. 2:11, Paul proclaims that he's not ignorant of Satan's schemes, and we shouldn't be either. When Satan tempts you to lust, he wants you to believe that it's no big deal. After you've sinned, he wants you to feel like you're the worst person on earth. Haven't you felt this way before after you sinned? The last thing you want to do is pray, read your Bible, or sing "Amazing Grace". You feel as if God has locked you in solitary confinement, and you don't get to come out for at least a few days. Certainly God doesn't want to hear how sorry you are, and you've promised not to do it again too many times...You are not worthy to enter the presence of the Lord.

I've got news for you: You never were worthy to begin with! Don't get me wrong, it is good to feel convicted when you sin, it is a proof of your spiritual vitality. But when the conviction turns to condemnation, you are playing into the enemy's hands. Outsmart him! If your own righteousness didn't qualify you to stand before God cleansed and forgiven in the first place, your current sin, no matter how great or redundant, can't disqualify you from His love and forgiveness. When you experience the awful guilt that sin produces, don't let it drive you away from God. Recognize the reality that the blood of Jesus is as powerful and effective on your worst days as it is on your best days. And let the guilt and disappointment of sin drive you to God, not away from Him. Be honest about your failure and frustration. But don't try to hide it. And don't let it keep you from God. Our time of greatest weakness is the time that we need Him most. His forgiveness for yesterday and His power and hope for today are available and sufficient.

Chapter 17

Wait To Say I Love You

When you make a vow to God, do not delay in fulfilling it. He has no pleasure in fools. Fulfill your vow. It is better not to vow than to make a vow and not fulfill it. Ecclesiastes 5:4-5 (NIV)

Words are important. Very important. They convey meaning, desire, fear, affection, emotion, and matters of the heart. They are the foundation of communication. There is no such thing as a meaningless or careless word.

Words can lift up or tear down. They can build or break. Words linger years after they leave the mouth. My grandparents could still remember specific things their grandparents said to them eighty years ago. Words never go away. They never disappear, and they always affect us in some way.

Why all the fuss over words? I believe it is in this area that many relationships become doomed before they ever get off the ground. The tendency in a relationship is to say too much too soon. Our hormones get cranked up, and all we know is that we are wildly attracted to a person, so we desire to express that attraction. Oftentimes before there is any physical contact or intimacy, there is a verbal intimacy that precedes it. Words pave the road, so to speak, that physical and sexual intimacy travel upon.

To prove my point, consider this example. What if someone asked me how I feel today and I responded by saying "I feel gay today!" My grandparents would have thought that I meant I feel happy, carefree, and lighthearted. You however would assume I meant homosexual. Words have meaning.

If you asked me to name some things that I love, I would list things like Wal-Mart, U2, collard greens, tractors, the Waffle House, and strong coffee from Starbucks. What if you said, "But Clayton, what about your wife and son?" Well of course I love them! But that is different. How is it different? I would not die for Wal-Mart, but I would lay my life down for Charie. If someone were trying to rob the Waffle House, not only would I not stop him or her, but also I would give him or her all my cash. However, if someone tried to harm my boy, I would do anything in my power to protect him, even if it meant harming him or her before they could hurt Jacob. The word love takes on an entirely new meaning depending on the context I use it in. Words have meaning.

Why does this matter in dating and marriage? Simply put, the words you say to one another have long-lasting effects and many times, they get your emotional motor racing. How many times have you laid in bed at night replaying conversations in your mind from the previous day? How often have we repeated phrases a guy or girl has said and tried to figure out what they really meant, some secret meaning or encrypted code? We call our friends to tell them what so and so said, then they comment on what they think it meant or what that person must have thought to have said such a thing.

This is an issue that I struggle with as a minister and preacher. I speak to a quarter of a million people a year, and that stage is a very lonely and vulnerable place. Every word I say has the potential to be taken in the wrong way or out of context by a large number of folks. And it happens! I recently made a joke about how I love to eat a big steak once a month, and a group of teenage vegetarians assaulted me afterwards, offended that I would be so cruel as to eat a cow or make them feel bad for only eating vegetables. That was not my intention, and I did not say that at all, but that is how they took it. (They were all wearing leather belts and shoes from dead cows, but they did not want to discuss that issue. They did not want to let the truth or the facts get in the way of their opinion).

When I first began preaching at age fourteen, my daddy told me "It does not matter what you say, or what you mean to say. It is what they hear you say that counts." I can get 100 compliments on a sermon and one negative remark, and I will dwell on the one negative remark for days, ignoring the others who were blessed and challenged. Words have meaning!

Have you ever been having a terrible day, and someone said something rude or mean to you, and it either made you break down in tears or want to punch his teeth out? On the other hand, have you ever had someone compliment you on how you look or a job you did, and that one compliment elevates your spirits for hours or even days? I sure have. Mark Twain said he could live a month off one good compliment.

So here's the deal; when we say deep, intimate words to each other before we are married, those words go deep down into our hearts. You may say something in the heat of the moment without much forethought, but the other person memorizes those words and will even bring them back up to you later, reminding you of what you said even though you may not have meant it that way. Recently a sixteen year-old girl at Crossroads camp told me that she and her boyfriend had already planned to be married when she finished high school. No offense, but I told her that was the most foolish and ill-advised thing they could do. You should NEVER even say the word marriage at that age, much less dwell on it and plan for it. That kind of conversation filled with those kinds of words only leads to heartache and regret.

In marriage, you must learn to speak carefully. I am still learning this, mostly from my mistakes. It is better to just wait and keep your mouth shut sometimes than to just say what you think. Once one person says a harsh word in a frustrated tone, the mood changes and the stakes are raised. Tempers begin to flare and tensions escalate. The bomb explodes.

But if one partner is mad and says something hurtful and the other listens calmly, or even apologizes with humility, the situation immediately settles. The bomb has been diffused. This takes character and patience and understanding, things that take years to develop through the power of the Holy Spirit.

The funny thing is, we very seldom ever keep the promises we make to one another when we are dating. You know it is true! Here are a few of the loaded words and phrases we swear to each other, only to break them all once we break up.

"I will always love you, forever and ever."
"I will always be there for you when you need me, no matter what happens."
"I will never love another person like this."
"I will wait for you, no matter how long it takes or how many miles separate us."
"You are the most beautiful person I have ever seen."
"I will never feel this way about anyone else as long as I live."
"I want to marry you and spend the rest of my life with you."
"I will never do you wrong or treat you bad."
"I will do anything to prove my love to you."

Oh, the theatrics and gymnastics we do with our words! These promises feel right at the time and sound as epic and honorable as a line from <u>Braveheart</u> or <u>Lord of the Rings</u>. But we all know that we cannot keep these promises. We don't even think about what we are saying before we say it. We just dive into the drama head first, and many of us break our necks because our words are deep but our intentions and abilities to keep them are simply too shallow. There is a time to say these things, and I have said all these things...TO MY WIFE. You should be a mature young adult who has decided in your heart that this is the person you are going to marry. You should be planning to follow through with marriage and making wedding plans, before you start spouting off at the mouth about undying love and eternal fidelity. In the words of my high school football coach, "Don't write checks with your mouth that you can not cash with your actions."

I can still remember the words I heard from a romantic interest in college. We were sitting on the steps of a building at Gardner-Webb on a cool autumn evening. The sun was setting, the crickets were chirping, and I think we both felt overwhelmed by the emotions of the moment. I knew that I wanted to date her and was clear about my intentions. She, on the other hand, was still hanging on to an old relationship, and I asked her where she stood. Her exact words as she gazed deep into my eyes were "Clayton King, you are an amazing man, and I just want to be with you." Wow! Exactly what I had wanted to hear! I leaned over and gave her an innocent kiss on the cheek. Nothing sexual took place, but her words had opened me up emotionally. The only problem was that she never followed through. Evidently she wanted to be with him too, because she never broke it off. I could not get her words out of my head. I would rewind and replay them, asking my friends what they thought she meant. Was she speaking in code? Was she a Navajo Windtalker?

Do you see how your words take you and the other person to places that you do not need to go until you have grown to know each other as friends and fellow believers? There are some things you should only say after you are engaged, and there other things you should only say after you are married. Your words may come back to haunt you so beware of what you say.

Since 1990 I have been speaking in public schools all over America about dating and relationships. I wish I had a dime for every girl who told me a tearjerker about a guy who pledged his heart and love to her for life. Then after he had sex with her and left her with an unwanted baby, he hit the bricks and never even called. I am not making this stuff up. Words have meaning,

Think of the *implications*.
Think of the *complications*.

And next time you want to bust out with something that sounds Shakespearean or John Donne-ish, ask yourself if you can cash that check you are writing with your mouth. If you can't, then keep your mouth shut.

As a smart person once said, "It is better to be thought a fool than to open your mouth and remove all doubt."

The brother of Jesus said it this way...
If anyone considers himself religious and yet does not keep a tight rein on his tongue, he deceives himself and his religion is worthless.
James 1:26 (NIV)

When you make a vow to God, do not delay in fulfilling it. He has no pleasure in fools. Fulfill your vow. It is better not to vow than to make a vow and not fulfill it. Ecclesiastes 5:4-5 (NIV)

Chapter 18

The Sex Connection

Flee from sexual immorality. All other sins a man commits are outside his body, but he who sins asexually sins against his own body. Do you not know that your body is a temple of the Holy Spirit, who is in you, whom you have received from God? You are not your own; you were bought at a price. Therefore honor god with your body. 1 Corinthians 6:18-20 (NIV)

You did not honestly think that we would attempt a book on love and dating without tackling this subject, did you?

Here is where I am going with this. I always tread carefully around this subject because our culture is so sex-crazed and sex-saturated. You cannot even say the word anymore without wondering about the various reactions from your audience. Therefore, I intend to treat it with respect, honesty, and bit of humor while not being crass or offensive. The bottom line is simple. Christians must deal with the subject of sexuality. The church has to begin teaching on this because few parents ever do. And if the people of God remain silent here, we will lose yet another generation of kids to a culture that wants to eroticize them at a young age so they can capitalize off of them for years to come. It is with this in mind that we revisit this issue from a Biblical perspective.

Here are some common myths perpetuated about sex.
It is normal to have sex before marriage.
If you are not sleeping with someone, you must be gay.
If you wear a condom, you won't get pregnant.
If you practice safe sex, you will not get AIDS.
You are justified in having sex if you love someone or like him or her a lot.
Sex is really no big deal, and everyone is doing it.
Sex is a great way to show someone you love him or her.

These and other incorrect beliefs about sexuality are destroying thousands of lives a day. I see them and talk to them every time I speak to teenagers or college students. I heard about it on my radio show from grown men who would call in, lamenting the loss of their jobs, wives, and children because of addictions to pornography. Sex is big business to some, but it needs to become serious business for you.

Here are a few correct ideas about sexuality.
God created sex, and it is not a sin in itself.
Sex is a great thing that two people enjoy in marriage.

Sex can be completely guilt free.
You can remain sexually pure for a lifetime, even after you are married.
You can be forgiven and restored when you mess up sexually.
Sex is not the most important thing in a marriage relationship.
You do not have sex all day long once you get married.

When two people decide to go beyond verbal intimacy, like we talked about in the last chapter, and they begin to explore physical intimacy with one another, it is like a car sliding on ice. You can put on the brakes, but it is nearly impossible to stop or control the vehicle. Sex and all that goes along with it are highly addictive to the human mind and body. Have you ever seen nude pictures? A sex scene in a movie? If you have, then you know exactly how difficult it is to erase those images from your mind. There is a sexual connection taking place, and I want to explain to you why this so important and why so many of us struggle with it.

There are hundreds of chemicals and millions of cells in the human body. At certain times our bodies release specific chemicals when they are needed. In situations with intense pain, like a wreck or an accident, the body will release endorphins. These are natural painkillers that work to keep you calm. They can even cause you to pass out. In stressful situations or times of great excitement, your body releases adrenaline. It gives you a sense of energy, a high of sorts. These are just two of the many chemicals God gave you, but they also do something else when released. They lock the particular experience in a part of your brain, and the memories remain forever, until another similar experience to the one that happened before happens again. Then the memories are triggered and the mind has a flashback. Old images resurface, old feelings return, even familiar sounds and smells are there. Drug users experience flashbacks frequently when they get high. War veterans experience combat flashbacks often. A Vietnam veteran who worked for my daddy for years would literally come unglued with uncontrollable shakes if a car backfired or if something fell on the floor with a loud noise. He took mortar fire for three days straight in the jungles of Vietnam, and those sounds triggered those chemicals, releasing those memories.

When you have a sexual experience, whether with someone or alone viewing pornography, those same chemicals are released and those memories are burned onto your hard drive. They stay there until triggered by a similar experience. Why do you think pornography in America is a multi-billion dollar industry? Why do you think it is so hard for couples to quit fooling around physically once they have started? The appetite of the flesh is relentless, and it wants more and more. That natural God-given desire is perverted and twisted until it cannot be satisfied.

A pastor once told me that he was married for ten months before he made love to his wife. I was confused and asked him why. He said that they had sex many times, but in his mind they were never alone. There were always other women in bed with them. They were his old lovers, and he was constantly having flashbacks of them while he was being intimate with his wife. He compared his wife to them, fantasized about them, and eventually had to go seek Christian counseling. By God's grace he overcame the struggle but still has to deal with those memories of regretted relationships and one-night stands.

If that scares you, then you are paying attention. This should be one of the most frightening realities you ever come face to face with. Sex is not a toy, and you cannot wear a condom on your heart. It is a deep, intimate, and complicated aspect of marriage between adults, not to be jumped into carelessly. Your sexual escapades will follow you for the rest of your life, so think about that before you make a decision that you will regret. One moment of pleasure is not worth a lifetime of pain.

Is it a sin to be tempted? Is it wrong to want to have sex? Absolutely not. It is normal and natural (I can hear many of you breathe a sigh of relief as you read those words). It is not a sin to be tempted because Jesus was tempted and He never sinned. It is wrong to give in to and follow it to destruction, and that is exactly where it leads. Get serious about being pure and guard your purity with your life. You will not regret it.

I praise God that I was a virgin on my honeymoon night and so was Charie. God gave us the strength to wait, but it was not easy. There was one situation I will never forget. I was on a date when I was seventeen with a very attractive girl that all my friends drooled over. It was just our third date, and we had not even kissed. We were going back to her house on a Saturday night in a rainstorm when all of a sudden, she took my hand, placed it in a very "private and personal" place on her body, and looked at me and said "Grab it like you want it!" (This was a popular song on the radio in 1990 and happened to be playing at that very moment). I did not know what to do! I did want to follow her orders, because I was a teenage boy who had zero experience with girls. But as my fleshed screamed YES my spirit screamed NO! I had visions of babysitting little junior on Saturday afternoons or going to the clinic to get medicine for herpes. I thought about college and having to tell my wife one day about this. But most of all I thought of Christ on the cross and how this would dishonor Him. I saw the ministry crumble and felt the sting of shame I would have to live with. I would lose all self-respect and disobey my Lord.

I did not plan it, but it just came out of me. Like a wildebeest on crack, giving birth, I screamed at the top of my lungs "NOOOOOO!" It scared us both, and she screamed too. I lost control of the car and we hydroplaned in the road. I thought I was dead. I saw the light at the end of the tunnel and heard grandma calling my name. I felt warm and shaky, like I was floating. Then all of a sudden the car came to a stop. We were not dead, just really scared. We stared at each other for a long time. I think she thought it was her fault. Then I finally broke the silence and said, "That was awesome! The hydroplaning thing, not the grab it like you want it thing." We drove the rest of the way home is silence, and I never saw her again. Pretty crazy, huh?

The point? We must train ourselves to react the right way when tempted, even when our bodies scream for sex or lust or sin. If we fail to learn this discipline, then we spiral out of control deeper and deeper into a sexual hole that we can't dig ourselves out of. Do you want to be a forty year-old woman who still regrets a high school relationship that went too far? Do you want to be a fifty year-old man and father of three who still flashes back in his mind to a college girlfriend when he is with his wife sexually?

These are serious considerations for you. The culture around you will throw every type of sin and temptation possible right in your face. Very few people will tell you to be pure and holy for God. Most voices you will hear in your life will influence you to let go of your convictions. Remove your boundaries. Forget your upbringing. Ignore religious leaders who want to strip you of exploring your sexuality. Indulge your appetite and do whatever feels good for the moment. There are no consequences, only unlimited amounts of sexual satisfaction! These are the lies you hear everyday and they are the very air you breathe.

But Jesus calls you to follow Him and to be a person of integrity and conviction, and His standard is the life He lived. The sexual connection belongs in marriage, protected by God and enjoyed by two people who have pledged a life to one another excluding everyone else on the planet. Any other sexual fantasy, relationship, or experience will stay with you for a lifetime, haunting you and reminding you that God's way is not only the right way, it is the best way for you to find true lifelong happiness without regret.

Chapter 19
How Far Is Too Far?

But among you there must not be even a hint of sexual immorality, or any kind of impurity, or of greed, because these are improper for God's holy people. Nor should there be obscenity, foolish talk, or coarse joking, which are out of place, but rather thanksgiving.
Ephesians 5:3-4 (NIV)

In the last seventeen years of traveling and speaking, the most common subject I am asked about is, without a doubt, relationships. And within that context, the most common question is "How far is too far?" I remember at a University here in NC when a young lady asked me how I defined sex. I was taken aback at first and asked her why she wanted to know. She was curious because she was doing everything with her boyfriend but intercourse, and in her mind, as long as they were not going "all the way" they were fine. Everything else was ok, as long as she could still call herself a virgin. This girl was a Christian and asked me this question after an evangelistic outreach.

Unfortunately, this seems to be the common opinion among most young Christians in their teens and twenties. Everyone from George Barna to James Dobson has said that the moral standards of church-going young people are no better at all than the morality of their peers who claim no faith at all and attend no church of any kind. Where does this disconnect come from?

This chapter is about boundaries but is about more than just setting boundaries that you hope you will be able to stay behind. We can never muster enough will power on our own to stick to our commitments. We must rely on the Holy Spirit to help us. That does not mean, however, that we should never even consider what is acceptable and reasonable in a relationship. If you fail to set boundaries and define lines in relationships, it is like trying to spear-fish with a q-tip. It will never work.

If your goal is simply to get as close as possible to the edge without going over it, then you are in trouble already. If all you want is to know what point of physical contact is sinful, then your desire is wrong. No matter where you try to draw a clear line, you will dance right up to it eventually, and more than likely you will cross it. The first time you break the boundary, you will feel guilty and ashamed. The next time you won't feel quite so bad, and by the third time, I guarantee you that you will have re-defined the boundary and moved further into the realm of sin to accommodate your own inability to stay within the lines.

Instead of asking, "How far is too far?", ask these questions:
What does God expect from me?

How can I please The Lord in this relationship?
How holy can I be?
How pure can I be for Christ?
Can I do this thing with pure motives and remain pure in mind and
heart afterwards?
Would I be ashamed to tell my spouse about this one day after we're married?

I remember as a child riding in the back seat of my mama's yellow 1975 Ford LTD. The backseat was the size of the Astrodome and my brother and I could have both had our own zip codes back there. But no matter where he sat, I wanted to touch him and aggravate him. And he wanted to hit and bother me, too. So mama had the brilliant idea to draw an imaginary line down the middle of the backseat. I had to stay left of center, and Brad had to stay right of center. I am sure it seemed like the thing to do at the time, but it lasted about as long as a donut at a cop convention.

Before she could even turn around, we were both seeing how close we could get to each other without crossing that imaginary line. That is the problem. All the lines we try to create in our relationships are imaginary. There are no real barbed wire or electric fences separating us from each other. If we purpose in our hearts to be pure, we will be pure. If we purpose in our hearts to experiment physically or indulge sexually, then we will find a way around any wall, roadblock, or boundary that we have set.

We must be true to what we know in our hearts is God's standard for us. We must be guided by His truth and standard or else we will be perpetually moving the line further and further away from safety and closer to sin and regret.

Can we hold hands?
Can we cuddle?
Can we kiss?
Can we French kiss (I actually prefer the new title of "Freedom" kiss)?
Can we remove clothing?
Can we lie on the couch together?
Can we go to co-ed sleepovers together?
Can we take naps together?

The list goes on and on (next thing you know someone is going to ask if they can bake homemade bread together while making out on the loveseat while watching <u>Trading Spaces</u>). When will this endless list of "Can I..." and "Is it ok if we..." ever end? Good grief!

A good rule of thumb is that if you have to ask whether or not it is ok, it is probably not ok. Notice we usually want to know if it is ok, not if it is right. We can justify and generalize things by convincing ourselves that they are ok, in other words they are not so bad. It's another debate when you move into the realm of what is right. Try asking "Is it right for you and me to cuddle (i.e.: spoon on the couch under the covers in the dark alone and get completely turned on knowing that we can not fulfill those desires that we just created by spooning on the couch under the covers in the dark alone?"). The passage in Philippians above gives us a filter that we can use when struggling with boundaries and limits.

Is it pure and right and honorable?
Could we do it with the lights on and not be ashamed?
Do you have to close the door to do it?
Would your parents or their parents be disappointed if they found out about it?
Is this the kind of action that would honor Jesus Christ?
Will I have to convince myself later that this was not really that bad?
Have I justified this because most everyone I know would be ok with it?

These are the kinds of questions we need to entertain if we authentically desire to live a life pleasing to God and pleasing to our future mate.

For a married couple the boundaries are clear. When you make the vow of marriage, it is a covenant between two people that is never to be broken. Speaking personally, I have some strict rules that I adhere to, not because I am legalistic, but because I do not want to be put into a tempting situation. I also fear the appearance of evil and losing a good testimony over something that could have been prevented.

I NEVER ride alone in a car with a woman unless it is my mother or my wife or a lady over the age of 178. Legalistic? No, just playing it safe. What would I be doing alone in cars with girls anyway? I have a truck and driver's license of my own.

I NEVER counsel a female alone under any circumstance. If a girl wants to talk to me after I speak, I make sure it is in a room with people in it and the lights on. I will never walk out of a room full of people with a female because I don't want a weaker brother or sister to wonder what we are doing leaving the room together.

I NEVER wind up alone with a woman in a room. I have literally found an excuse to leave a classroom or a meeting room when I realized it was just myself and another female. "Oh, I am sorry, it is time for me to go take my Hydrochromyoxydone injections for my Slovakian encephalitis" or something like that.

I NEVER go out to lunch alone with a young lady, even if it is in a conspicuous place. Someone asked me once if I had a hard time trusting myself, and my answer was a solid and definitive YES. Of course I don't trust myself. Do you trust yourself? You are crazy if you do. Many people have lost their marriages by convincing themselves that they would "never do anything like have an affair or cheat on my mate." So do I intend or plan on having an affair? No I don't, and that is the point. I PLAN. As Steinbeck said, and I paraphrase, the best laid plans of mice and men often go astray. So if you are going to plan, plan to never be in a situation where you could be tempted.

I NEVER spend more than a few minutes on the phone with women just to be careful. I am not rude about it, but I don't trust my heart and I don't trust people that I don't know. Lots of married men have told me that the one thing women seem the most attracted to them about is their wedding ring. There are men and women out there just looking for a marriage to wreck. I want to protect mine at any cost. I just want to be extremely careful so that no one could ever even make an accusation. Billy Graham was so cautious that he would not ride on an elevator alone with a woman, and he sent people into his hotel rooms before he would enter to make sure nothing and no one had been planted there. Look at the legacy and testimony he has had for Christ!

You may think I am psychotic and over the top about this. But honestly, I do not care what you think. I am not married to you. I am married to Charie. You did not save me, Jesus did. So my allegiance is to my wife, my son, and my Savior. If the three of them are pleased with me, then what everyone else thinks about me is quite frankly the least of my concerns. I would rather err on the side of holiness than to be nonchalant and let my guard down. If I truly love my family, then is there any length I would not go to or any price I would not pay to guard our relationship?

For the unmarried person, things are a bit different. The standard is still purity and holiness, but since you have not already made the marriage covenant, it fleshes itself out a bit differently, since you are still single, available, and perhaps looking for the right one. I personally am not against dating as a whole. I know that some people are and that is fine, but I feel it a tad legalistic to call all dating sinful and destructive. Charie and I dated and it was glorious! Not every dating relationship ends up turning both parties into depressed Psycho-Billy-Ninjas who want to do mean things to each other's pets.

What I am against is immature and selfish relationships that ruin people emotionally. I don't believe it is the entity of dating that is evil and destructive. I believe it is the motivation and maturity of the people dating that makes it or breaks it. And please don't try to use the argument that dating was never in the Bible so we should not do it. Guess what other groovy things are not in the Bible? Cars, fast food, church buildings, family life centers, Christian bookstores, and emergency rooms. Are you going to go sell your truck because Paul did not have one? No way. If I get shot, I am going to the ER whether or not there was one in 1st century Jerusalem. Again, I think that it is the maturity level and spirituality of the people involved that make it a good idea or a catastrophe.

If you are not married but want to be, then live your life like you plan to be married one day to the man or woman of your dreams, because one day you will be and that day will be here before you can say, "boo." Allow the Holy Spirit to fill your life so much that you would not dare do things physically or sexually that would hurt God or you or your future mate. Study the scriptures and live off of the principles you find there, testing every thought, idea, and motivation by the Word of God. And stay far, far away from the edge. Do not dance on the precipice of the cliff of sexual sin because you will fall. That fire will burn you. As the scriptures ask, can a man scoop hot coals onto his lap and not be burned? Of course not. Your best bet is to keep your mind on Christ and your hands to yourself until you are married. Then, get some Gatorade, put it in high gear, and make up for all those years you waited with the one you waited for!

Section Three

Red Flags (Chapters 20-30)

Instruct a wise man and he will be wiser still;
Teach a righteous man and he will add to his learning.
Proverbs 9:9 (NIV)

I believe that if you will learn to notice the little things, paying attention to small details, you can avoid the drama and hurt that accompanies so many relationships. There are warning signs that you need to be aware of, and I call them "Red Flags". They are there for anyone to see and they are there for your benefit; to keep you from making a drastic mistake that you will regret someday. It takes little discernment to see these red flags, but it takes lots of guts to back off once you are aware of them. This entire section of the book is loaded with common sense and practical approaches to saving your marriage before it ever gets started.

The first step is to stay away from the wrong kinds of people so that you don't marry the wrong kind of person. We need to be more deliberate about our relationships instead of casually shooting in the dark. Pay attention and learn from the mistakes of others, and pay attention to the red flags. Here are just a few examples of what I am talking about:

Does this person have a short fuse? Is this person easily angered?
How does he treat his parents? Is he disrespectful and mean to them?
Do others respect her, or does she have a bad reputation?
Does he have any bad habits that I cannot stand, or could not live with?
Is there always a major crisis going on in his or her life?
Has she had many serious relationships before me? Why did they end?
Has he had many short relationships before me? Why did they end?
Do I have a warning or uneasy feeling in my heart about this person?
Do my parents disapprove or have reservations about this person?
Do we disagree on politics or our religious beliefs?
Do we agree on what a family is supposed to be?
Do we disagree about who leads the family or how to discipline kids?
Do we have different desires concerning money and material possessions?
Will our desired careers conflict with each other or compliment each other?
Am I comfortable with his or her physical and sexual history in past relationships?
Am I constantly doubting this relationship and questioning whether it's right?
Do I feel like this person is lying to me or hiding things at times?
Does she constantly put herself down or say she is fat, ugly, or stupid?
Does he get jealous and possessive when I spend time with other friends?
Is she obsessed with her body or her appearance?

Does he put other people down in public or make fun of others?
Is she conceited or arrogant?
Does he listen to me and treat me with kindness and respect?

Go ahead and get over the fear of feeling like you are constantly questioning and criticizing the other person. Forget that feeling of "Who am I to ask all these questions?" Learn to guard your heart by asking the right kinds of questions and paying attention to the little things. People usually don't change on their own. It takes God to change someone, so by paying attention now, you will be able to tell what kind of person he will be when he is married. Just multiply their habits and traits they have now by ten and that is the person you will be married to in ten years. If you see stuff you hate now, I would not bet on those things changing after marriage.

Of course relationships require risks. No one will ever be perfect, and no one will ever meet your perfect expectations. We must be willing to overlook mistakes and character flaws, but at some point you need to draw the line and say, "There are just too many red flags here."

Most of us ask more questions about the used car we want to buy than about the person we are dating. That is just plain dumb. You will either uncover this stuff before you get involved, or trust me, you will find it out after you are already in the relationship!

This final section of the book will go into greater detail about the questions listed above and why it is so important to use common sense and pay attention to red flags when you see them.

Chapter 20

Spiritual Inequality

Do not be bound together with unbelievers; for what partnership have righteousness and lawlessness, or what fellowship has light with darkness? 2 Corinthians 6:14 (NASB)

A strong word of advice: don't date dead people. Ephesians 2:1 describes the condition of the person who does not know Jesus Christ as Savior and Lord: they are "dead in trespasses and sins". When I'm asked if it's okay for Christians to date non-Christians, I answer the question with a question: "Is it okay for a living person to date a dead person?" That usually gets the point across. So here it is, in print for the sake of posterity, a statement I will defend until my dying day: A Christian should never-never-ever date a non-Christian. That should be basic to our instincts as children of God, but you'd be surprised how many students make this costly mistake. Usually, the Christian convinces his or herself that they can convert the prospective boyfriend or girlfriend, or show them the love of Christ by dating them. I sarcastically refer to this as "missionary dating". Let me save you tons of time, heartache, and unnecessary temptation: missionary dating is not effective. Almost always, the Christian begins a slow and steady spiritual decline as the relationship progresses.

Compromise is inevitable in this situation because the two people operate according to two different realities and worldviews. For the Christian, God is the center of every decision. For the non-Christian, temporal pleasures and successes are the chief goals of life. How can this relationship work? It can't. Even if the non-Christian becomes saved in the process of the relationship, this type of dating is not justified. If God is sovereign, He can save the non-Christian without a Christian compromising his or her values to date the person. He doesn't need our romantic evangelism to speed up the process. In fact, the best witness that a non-Christian can see is a Christian strong enough to stick to her values in a non-judgmental way. It will demonstrate Christ in a powerful way to an unbeliever for you to explain, "I'm sorry, but I can't date someone who doesn't have a real and growing relationship with God. It wouldn't be fair to either of us, and it would be hypocritical of me. But I'm happy to be your friend." It makes your faith appear anemic and weak for you to settle for a relationship with an individual who doesn't belong to Your God.

Now we turn to a more blurry scenario-how about two Christians who are in different stages of their walks with God? Can a strong Christian date a weaker Christian? Should a Christian who has been serving God for years date a brand new Christian? These are valid questions, and the answers aren't clearly defined. To begin with, we are all at different stages of our walks with God. Furthermore, God doesn't grade our spirituality on a human scale-it's not like some of us are A+ Christians and others rate as an unimpressive C-. With that said, spiritual inequality is a serious red flag in a dating relationship. Although it is impossible to establish definitive criteria for what spiritual equality looks like, I think the following are obvious signs that two Christians who are considering dating each other should be very careful.

You might be in a spiritually unequal relationship if:

1. The other person never seems to want to go to church, or at church, is preoccupied with everything but God. This could include talking during music, passing notes, etc.
2. The other person has been a Christian for a while but remains pretty ignorant of the Word of God and the basics of Christianity.
3. The person never wants to talk about spiritual things, or accuses you of being a Jesus freak when you want to talk about the Lord.
4. The person is ashamed of his or her faith, and won't take a stand for Christ around his or her friends or people he or she wants to impress.
5. The person is always pushing you to step outside of God's boundaries physically and sexually.
6. The person is involved in a lot of questionable activities and claims that God understands, or it's no big deal. Often this includes hanging out with people who are getting drunk or using drugs.

Above all, if you are constantly having to convince yourself that it's okay to be in a dating relationship with someone, you are probably arguing with the Holy Spirit. It breaks my heart to see a believer who is sold out to the purposes of the Kingdom of God become tangled up in a dating relationship with a half-hearted Christian. When I was in high school, two young ladies gave their lives to Christ at a Fellowship of Christian Athletes meeting. They were very serious and sincere in this profession of faith, but they both had boyfriends who were nominal Christians at best. I watched with sadness as both of the young ladies refused to end their dating relationships, and their spiritual lives were ruined as a result. Their boyfriends didn't understand why the girls wanted to bring their Bibles to school, or why they didn't feel comfortable being alone as a couple in tempting situations anymore. Eventually, the young ladies gave in to the lukewarm pseudo religion of their complacent boyfriends. This is the norm. When one Christian is pursuing God with all of his or her heart and the other Christian in the relationship is stagnant and apathetic about spiritual matters, slow disaster will be the result.

What is the rule of thumb for deciding whether you are on the same page with someone spiritually? In a way, I think you just know. But when your emotions blind you and confuse the issue, look at the facts. Is this person growing in his relationship with Jesus? Is he consistent? Is he humble enough to learn and be molded by God? Do I see this person responding daily to the activity of God in his life? Ask questions of the person, such as "What have you been reading in the Bible lately?" If they stutter and stammer and can't really think of anything when this question is presented, be careful. Ask the person to share his testimony with you. If he doesn't seem genuine and certain about his personal walk with God, evaluate the relationship again.

It's hard to exercise discernment in this area without developing a judgmental attitude. I am not advising you to pick a person apart and demand perfection from the next person you date (unless you want to be single for a really long time!) I'm glad my wife overlooked many of my flaws and decided she'd put up with me because she loved me. However, she had no doubt that we both desired God's complete and total rule in our lives, and that outweighed my quirks, bad habits, and sinful tendencies. As I shared in an earlier chapter, I know firsthand the misery that results when one person tries to drag along the dead weight of a spiritually lazy and ambivalent believer in a dating relationship. When you date someone, you are connected to that person to a degree. You are affiliating yourself with her, and you are going to reflect her and give your heart to her in many ways. It is a serious thing to devote yourself exclusively to another person. And if that other person isn't determined to love God with all of his heart, soul, mind and strength, you're headed for utter frustration.

I'll conclude with a plea. If you are the spiritually weaker partner in a relationship, are you aware that you will be accountable to God if you bring that person down or hinder that person from growing up to maturity in Christ? I beg you to back out of the relationship until you are more stable in your walk with God. If you are the stronger member of the relationship and several of the warning signs I have mentioned are present in the other person, you are flirting with severe danger. If you continue to give your heart to someone who doesn't desire the glory of God as life's ultimate treasure, if you settle for someone who's barely getting by spiritually, you could very well end up in an agonizing marriage. The spiritual gap may widen over the years, and it can affect every component of your life, including how your kids are raised and the major decisions you make about life direction. At that point, it will be too late to heed the warning signs, because marriage is for life. Please evaluate your potential or current significant other in the revealing light of God's Word, and don't compromise your standards. Don't fill your future with inevitable regret.

Chapter 21
Immaturity & Indecision

We have much to say about this, but it is hard to explain, because you are so slow to learn. In fact, though by this time you ought to be teachers, you need someone to teach you the elementary truths of God's word all over again. You need milk, not solid food! Anyone who lives on milk, being still an infant, is not acquainted with the teaching about righteousness. But solid food is for the mature, who by constant use have trained themselves to distinguish good from evil. Hebrews 5:11-14 (NIV)

I sat there for about an hour listening to her talk about this guy. The story was at times funny, at other times entertaining, but mostly sad.

There she was. A beautiful nineteen year-old college freshman. She was at one of the leading universities in America and was in the pre-med program. Her dream was to become a doctor and travel the world as a medical missionary. She had already been to seven countries and felt God call her while in Haiti at age sixteen. She had never dated seriously in high school because of church, sports, and school. You could tell that she had it all together. She was the total package for most any guy. She was mature and well spoken. She made eye contact when she talked. Her manners were impeccable and she was both sweet and genuine. She was a college boy's dream.

Then there was "him". I never met "him", but I felt like I knew "him" after sixty minutes of listening to her brutal story.

They met at freshman orientation. He was a rising junior who would graduate early. There was an automatic chemistry that developed between them from the first conversation. They would look for each other every day and end up eating together in the cafeteria together. They would talk for hours about home, their parents, and their dreams in life. She fell for him.

He asked her out, and they had a fantastic date; dinner at a fine restaurant, coffee afterwards, and long walk in the park followed by feeding ducks at sunset. I have to admit I was impressed by how smooth this guy was.

On their fourth date he told her that he had been praying about their relationship and felt like God had told him they needed to date and pursue marriage. She felt good about it and had always wanted a guy who would be a leader, pursue her, and make decisions. One thing led to another, and they wound up dating exclusively for her whole freshman year. She was not bothered by the slight age difference since it was only two years, and she loved his leadership in the relationship.

At about six months she noticed a change in his demeanor towards her. They had already shared so much and had even talked about what they wanted in a marriage, how many kids each wanted, and whether or not their careers were compatible. It was the new stage of love where everything is wonderful and love conquers all and "who needs money or food as long as we have each other" kind of thing. But as the freshness wore off, he began to act a little funny. She noticed but tried to ignore it.

Then all of a sudden one day he woke her up with a phone call and informed her that he had been acting distant because God was dealing with him about some things, and God had told him to break up with her. She thought it was a joke and laughed but he told her he was dead serious. When she asked for a reason, he said he could not focus on God and her at the same time. He needed to sacrifice her to God and spend more time with The Lord, reading the Word and praying and making a priority of his relationship with Jesus. He did not have time for both of them.

A week later, he came by her apartment in tears. He told her he had made a mistake, and he wanted her back. It was all wrong, and he didn't realize what he had until her let her go. He begged for another chance and even said that God had given him a peace about them being together. She listened and reluctantly agreed to give it another try and see how things went. They began having Bible studies together and praying each night on the phone before bed. She felt like things were progressing in a positive way, and she said she could really see herself marrying him.

Then, at the end of the school year, totally out of the blue and without warning, he broke up with her again. This time he blamed God and himself. He said he did not know what he wanted. He was graduating soon and had no idea what he wanted in the way of a career or if he even wanted to graduate. It was not a problem with her. It was a problem with him. God did not want him to be in a relationship with her if he himself was unsure of what he wanted. It would not be fair to her to keep her hanging on to something with no guarantee. He needed some time alone, single and without a girlfriend, to find God and seek His will without distraction.

So they had the break-up talk and went home for the summer. She went on a mission trip to Jamaica and had a great summer getting over him, but still hoping that things might work out next semester. Then she moved back to college.

The first day back she was going to buy books and turned a corner. She ran right into her ex-boyfriend (the one who had been told by God to stay single so he could focus on Christ). And he was not alone. He was with a girl, and they were holding hands (insert awkward feeling here). She said she just stared at the two of them for a few seconds, then turned and ran back to her room where she cried for a long, long time.

"I am so confused by this. How could God tell him we were supposed to date and get married? Then God told him to break up with me. Then God told him he had made a mistake, and we needed to date again. Then God told him he wasn't ready for a relationship, and he needed to be single. Did God tell him to dump me for the other girl?"

This conversation happens all the time because this kind of thing happens all the time. God was not telling that guy anything. He was blaming God because he was immature and indecisive. Let me say it again for clarity.

God was not telling him anything.
He was immature.
He was indecisive.
He did not know what he wanted.
He wanted two different girls at two different times.
He blamed God for his own immaturity.
He deeply hurt a precious young lady with his indecisiveness.
God got the blame, but it was not God's fault.
It was his fault.

The bottom line here is that he was right. He was not ready for commitment at all and should have never gotten involved in the first place. That is usually the case but we rush ahead anyway governed by our hormones or immaturity or insecurity instead of being ruled by self-control and the Holy Spirit.

Why do so many people follow this pattern in relationships? Maybe we just do not know any better. Maybe we assume that we cannot do any better. Maybe we are so desperate for a relationship that we would rather have one that is dysfunctional and destructive than not have one at all. Maybe we learned it from television or the movies, or maybe even from watching our friends change boyfriends or girlfriends more than they change clothes. Either way, this roller-coaster ride seems to be the rule instead of the exception, and it is filling people's hearts and lives with emotional baggage that they will carry with them for the remainder of their days if they do not stop the vicious cycle of indecision.

How can you avoid this cycle and guard your heart from this kind of thing? Perhaps the place to start is inside. Look into your heart and take inventory of your life. Do you consider yourself a mature person? Here are a few questions to ask before taking the plunge into a relationship. These can be applied to both you and the person you are thinking about dating or marrying.

These questions, if answered honestly, will give you insight into the maturity level of you and the person you are interested in.

Does he or she start things without finishing them?
How many romantic relationships has he or she been involved in during the last two years?
Why did they end? What happened?
How is he with money? Does he spend more than he makes?

Was she or is she spoiled?
Does he always expect to get what he wants?
How does she respond when she doesn't get her way?
Is she constantly surrounded by unnecessary drama?
Does he create drama out of every situation?
How much time does he spend watching TV daily?
How much money does he or she owe? Car payment, credit card, etc.?
How much time does he spend on the computer or playing video games?

Some of you are thinking, "I would never ask those questions! They are way too personal and those things are none of my business." If that is your attitude, then you are speeding towards disaster and you will be broken hearted and frustrated in no time flat.

Please hear me on this. You MUST ask these questions. This is our problem. We treat relationships like they are no big deal, but they are literally the most important things in life! So get over the fear or timidity that you are feeling and start dealing with the reality of life: half of all people who are married today get divorced, mostly because they never consider the enormity of the decision they make in matrimony. Rush in and then rush out. Families are split, kids are devastated, and our culture spirals into an abyss of moral relativism all because people feel like it is none of their business to ask questions like this. If someone wants to get involved with you and you are considering letting him or her into your life in an intimate way, then you are foolish and naive to ignore these questions! If you don't ask up front, I promise that you will end up asking later, when you have already invested time and effort into a relationship you are beginning to have doubts about.

I would want to know if I were dating someone who was extremely indecisive! I would never want to date someone whose average relationship lasted three months. If a guy can't stay with a girl for more than a month and that is a consistent pattern, you would be wise to find that out and avoid him. That's right, I said it, AVOID HIM. Do not be casual about something as important as the rest of your life. This is your heart and your future! If the person you like is immature and indecisive, then walk away. Either you are not ready or they are not ready. One day the time will be right, but it is not your job to bring that person to maturity, and it is not his or her job to raise you. You will both eventually grow and mature, and at that point, the timing may be right. Just because someone is immature and cannot make up his mind about who or what he wants does not mean he is a bad person. He may be a great person, but just not ready for the effort it takes to make a relationship work.

You are better off waiting a little longer until both parties are settled and sure of who they are and what they want. Love is a decision, and if you are incapable of making it for a lifetime, you are not ready. Wait, and remember that among the many things we can say about love, it is most certainly patient.

Chapter 22
Selfishness, Vanity, & Materialism

But Jesus called them to Himself and said, "You know that the rulers of the Gentiles lord it over them, and their great men exercise authority over them. It is not this way among you, but whoever wishes to become great among you shall be your servant, and whoever wishes to be first among you shall be your slave; just as the Son of Man did not come to be served, but to serve, and to give His life a ransom for many." Matthew 20:25-28 (NASB)

I never knew how selfish I was until I got married. They say this awareness will multiply exponentially when I become a father. That's scary. Because of our sinful condition, selfishness is our natural disposition. Selfishness causes you to roll your eyes when your parents ask you to take out the trash. It causes you to get in a knock down drag out fight with your younger sibling about whose turn it is to do the dishes. Selfishness is at the root of the great American question: "What's in it for me?"

I'm in a sticky situation here. I need to tell you to beware if you are considering dating a person who has many selfish tendencies. Yet I have I seen in my own life a sickening degree of selfishness which has not yet been overcome by the authority of the Holy Spirit. However, I am progressing and being conformed to the selfless image of Christ daily. Please remember that these red flags are intended to help you evaluate yourself first, and then to evaluate your relationship. With that in mind, are you a selfish person? Of course, on some levels you are-we all are! But deep down, are you consumed with selfishness, or are you striving to replace ego centricity with Christ centrality? Again, I've developed a brief checklist for you to evaluate how you're doing in the struggle against selfishness.

Selfish People:
1. Always talk about themselves
2. Are more concerned with their reputation than the feelings or needs of others.
3. Never sacrifice money, time, or opportunities for recognition in order to help others.
4. Have an unhealthy preoccupation with material things.
5. Place an inordinate amount of attention on how they and other people look and dress.
6. Resent being asked to do anything that is a slight inconvenience.
7. Get their feelings hurt very easily when they are overlooked or misunderstood.

These are certainly just a few indications of selfishness. And we all cringe a little at certain points of this list because we know we're guilty. But let me assure you: people who are consumed with themselves make terrible boyfriends or girlfriends, and even worse husbands and wives. Some of the most prominent displays of the self-centeredness of current American culture are the commercials and marketing schemes used to convince us to buy products. If I hear another advertiser tell me that "I deserve it" or "I have the right to..." or "It's time to put myself first" I think I'm going to be sick. More and more Christians seem to be buying into this selfish worldview which features them as an individual at the center of their own personal universe. I assure you that nothing is more miserable than dating a person who thinks the world revolves around them. Actually there is something more miserable than dating a person like this: being a person like this!

The great irony of selfishness is that, like so many other sins, it delivers the exact opposite of what it promises. By being selfish we expect to get ahead, to find fulfillment, and to take care of ourselves. After selfishness has run its course, we find that we've actually fallen behind, come up empty, and destroyed ourselves. Selfishness is a tricky thing to pinpoint, and sometimes it even masks itself as spirituality. On one occasion, Jesus carefully explained to the disciples that the time was drawing near for Him to be mocked, scourged, and crucified. James, John, and their mother decided to capitalize on this opportunity to ask Jesus for a special place in the Kingdom. I know it seems asinine that they would dare ask for personal favors in a context like this, but their selfishness isn't much different than ours. We live in the present reality of the accomplishments and benefits of the sacrificial work of Christ, and we have the audacity to be selfish? We frequently seek honor, prestige and glory for ourselves at the expense of the glory of God and the ministry of the gospel. We've learned to put ourselves first and to pat ourselves on the back for doing so.

Jesus quickly corrected James, John, and their mama, and explained to all of the disciples what a true Kingdom paradigm looked like:

> But Jesus called them to Himself and said, "You know that the rulers of the Gentiles lord it over them, and their great men exercise authority over them. It is not this way among you, but whoever wishes to become great among you shall be your servant, and whoever wishes to be first among you shall be your slave; just as the Son of Man did not come to be served, but to serve, and to give His life a ransom for many."
> Matthew 20:25-28 (NASB)

This is entirely opposite the world's perspective. In fact, it seems upside down. It seems backwards. Jesus not only taught this truth, He embodied it. He came to live as a man, and He poured His life out for the sake of His creation. True Christ-likeness must be built on the foundation of selflessness.

If you really desire a relationship without regret, you must submit to this essential truth: IT'S NOT ABOUT YOU! When two people enter a relationship with the primary intention of getting their own needs met, they end up disillusioned and disenchanted. Years later, they often end up divorced. Take a look at your current internal life. Are you ready to put the needs and wants of another person above your own needs and wants? This is an easy thing to do in the beginning stages of a relationship because each person is focused on impressing the other. However, when the glamour fades away, selfishness often settles in. If you are not ready to love a person when they're unlovable and serve the person even when they take it for granted, you're not ready for a committed relationship. You should begin to ask God to give you a heart like Jesus, who "emptied Himself, taking the form of a bond-servant, being made in the likeness of men." Philippians 2:7 (NASB) And if you are in a relationship with someone who seems to use you for his own pleasures, or seems to use others to get what he wants, you should get out immediately. This selfishness will only get worse and more obvious as time goes on.

I want to reiterate that we're all selfish in many ways, and God is still working on all of us. Further, there are some ways in which being married is knocking some of the selfish edge off of me in a way that singleness could not. I'm sure having kids will hasten this process even more! However, it is dangerous to allow unchecked, unacknowledged selfishness to exist in a relationship. Since pride is the root of selfishness, it is a serious offense to God. And since humility is the beginning of true wisdom, selfishness will stunt your spiritual growth faster than almost anything else. Take this warning seriously: selfishness is not okay, and it must be eliminated gradually by the power of God. When you remember that He is your Creator, and you belong to Him, it makes selfishness look as ridiculous as it is. And it makes giving yourself away to God and others a true pleasure.

Chapter 23

Bad Reputation

A good name is more desirable that great riches; to be esteemed better than silver or gold. Proverbs 22:1 (NIV)

I grew up in a small town. Actually, I did not grow up in town at all. I grew up miles outside the city limits on a farm where I could ramble in the woods, build forts, hunt and fish, and pick blackberries. I am thankful for the way and the place I was raised, for it has shaped and formed not only my life, but the life of my little boy as I attempt to provide for him all the good things my parents provided for me.

Back to my point...my hometown of Fountain Inn, SC, was relatively small and word traveled fast. There was a genuine lack of privacy and discretion, because you either knew everyone or were related to them. This had a good side to it. There was actually a sense of community. You knew your neighbors and sat with them on the porch having actual conversations about meaningful things. If I were caught misbehaving at church or in public by one of my friend's parents, they had every right to discipline and spank me as my own parents did. My parents wanted them to. And they did not threaten to have them arrested either. Of course my parents did the same to my friends, and everyone expected and appreciated the willingness of the community to collectively help raise children. Hilary Clinton at least had a good title to her book It Takes a Village. In my experience, it took a village (full of parents with hickory switches and leather belts).

The downside of the small town is gossip. Everyone knows everyone and their business, too. It is not called slander or gossip. It is simply referred to as "sharing a prayer request."

If you have ever had a rumor spread about you that was not true, you know how devastating it feels. You go through a thousand questions. Who started it? Who all did they tell? Do I confront them about it? I wonder if everyone thinks it is true? There is nothing worse that having people spread lies about you.

Recently this happened to me. My closest friend, with whom I am co-authoring this book, told me that a student at his college was telling people that he heard me curse once in a sermon. Steven asked me if it was true, and I informed him that I had never cursed in a sermon in my life. Even when I preached from the King James Version and came across the word a** I substituted the word donkey (I will not even *type* the word). So he went to the guy spreading the rumor, and he defended me, telling him to stop spreading the lie and to correct it with anyone he had gossiped to. What a good friend!

However, sometimes we need to stop and listen when someone is consistently spoken of by others in a negative light. There may be a reason some people have a bad reputation. If the people who warn you about someone are mature, strong Christians who don't make it a habit to slander people for no reason, then that may be a warning you should at least consider.

This is not an excuse or a license to injure people or to listen to slander about people. But as Proverbs 22:1 warns us, we should desire a good name. A good reputation goes a long way because your reputation precedes you wherever you go and it lingers behind after you have gone. So if you find yourself attracted to someone or even dating him or her but all you hear about him or her is negative, then you need to investigate. It may be totally false. It may also be completely true. You will never know until you practice caution by investigating.

When I started public school in the tenth grade at Hillcrest High, the first day of class I received a letter in my locker from a junior. She informed me that she had been to our Jamboree football game the previous week and thought I was cute. She wanted to get to "KNOW ME" (and she had capitalized it and put it in quotes just like that). I was pretty surprised. I had just come from a Christian school to play football, and I was the new guy at a school of 1400 students, and an older girl I had never met wanted to go out with me! I was so innocent and clueless.

So after school, I went to the locker room to get ready for football practice and of course, I had to tell all the guys that this girl liked me. They all laughed and made fun of me until I showed them the letter. As soon as they saw the name of the girl, they immediately told me to throw the letter away and stay away from her. When I asked why, they told me that she wasn't the kind of girl a Christian like me needed to be messing with. The irony was that none of those guys were believers! But they were looking out for one of their own, and I figured I should be careful. It was not that I thought I was better than her, but as a Christian and a young preacher, I wanted to practice Proverbs 22:1 and guard my name. It would have been a bad mistake for me to pursue it if I thought it would harm my testimony for Christ.

I believe that is where many of us get confused. We think it is mean or judgmental to make a decision not to date someone based on his or her reputation because who are we to judge?

Let me explain something that needs to be clarified. There is a huge difference in "making a judgment" and "passing judgment." When I wake up in the morning and it is cloudy and the wind is blowing and the weatherman is calling for rain, I make a judgment. I decide I think it is going to rain so I take a raincoat and umbrella. I am a fool if I go through life never making judgments. We do it every day, whether deciding if we will buy stock in a company or buying gas at Texaco because it is cheaper than Exxon. We must make judgments.

Passing judgment is different. It means that we set ourselves up in place of God by trying to know the motives of someone's heart and judging whether or not they are saved by Christ. We are forbidden to do that because only Christ can pass judgment on people. That is what the book of Revelation is all about; Jesus Christ coming to make righteous and true judgments pertaining to what people have done and how they have lived. So when it comes to someone with a bad reputation, use discernment and judge whether or not you should move ahead. A bad reputation is an immediate red flag.

You are not judging him or her. You are judging the situation.

If I moved to a new city and asked ten people what was the best Mexican restaurant in town and one said Pedro's and nine said Monterrey's, wouldn't you think it odd if I went to Pedro's?

Some people choose to ignore the warnings of a person with a bad name and go ahead with it. I won't drag you through any of the number of stories I could tell you about people who wish they would have listened and proceeded with more caution. Many times, where there is smoke there is fire. Find out why someone has a bad name before you blindly dive in. Don't be afraid to ask questions, but be prepared to make a tough decision to abort the mission if the rumors prove true.

Other people seem to be attracted by guys or girls with a bad rep. I have never figured this one out when it comes to girls. Now guys, that I can understand. There are some guys who only want sex, so they set out on a mission to find girls who will "put out." They seek out girls with a bad rep. That was the daily conversation in the locker room at high school (and if the girls who did give in to their boyfriends knew half of what they said about them behind their backs, they would never speak to them again).

With girls though, there seems to be certain kind of female that thrives off dating guys who just use women. They seem to like being ignored or abused and the worse a guy will treat them, the more loyal they become to him. Certain psychologists say it is the mothering instinct in some women. Others call it the "messiah complex."

It is when a girl wants to fix and save the bad boy. Anyway you name it, it is co-dependency, and it can happen to guys, too. There are those who want to date someone with a bad rep and terrible life skills because it makes them feel needed and important; someone needs them in their life, and it feels good to be needed.

Here are some questions you need to ask when you find yourself interested in someone who has developed a bad reputation.

How many people share this opinion of him or her?
Are these trustworthy people saying these things?
Is there someone I can ask to validate these rumors?
Am I willing to take the chance that the rumors may be true?
*Am I willing to risk my reputation on this relationship that may not
    even work?*

Why don't I just go straight to the person I like and ask him about the rumors?

What do my parents think about my dating someone with this kind of reputation?

If I knew the rumors were true, would I date her anyway?

We check references for jobs. We check references for home loans and automobile loans. We have to apply for a credit card. We have to apply for admission to college. These things, in the long run, are nowhere near as important as the person you are going to marry and have children with. Check his or her references, unless you just don't care at all about what kind of person you grow old with. The goal is to be married until death and grow old together. If you ignore the red flag of a bad reputation, there is a good chance that you will never get that chance.

Chapter 24

Insecurity & Jealousy

Do not be anxious about anything, but in everything, by prayer and petition, with thanksgiving, present your requests to God. And the peace of God, which transcends all understanding, will guard your hearts and your minds in Christ Jesus. Philippians 4:8-9 (NIV)

I have already told you how Charie and I met. It was one of the top three moments of my life. The first time we spoke that night at UNC, when she approached me and asked about working at Crossroads, there was one thing that stood out beyond all of her good qualities. To be sure, she was beautiful. I take that back, she was actually drop-dead-on-the-spot-gorgeous. She took my breath away. But it wasn't really her physical beauty that struck me. It was her sense of security in who she was.

Charie was not trying to impress me. She did not begin to rattle off lots of statistics about her spiritual pilgrimage. She was not interested in telling me how many countries she had been to or how long she had known the Lord. She had this quiet sense of identity that I just knew could not be shaken.

I did not impress Charie. She was not blown away, and I mean that in a good way. Often times people compliment me after a message and say things like, "God really used you" or my favorite, "I really enjoyed that." (Sometimes that's good, but sometimes I worry that if too many people are enjoying my sermons that maybe I am doing something wrong!). Charie, however, did not compliment or encourage me in any way. Now don't get the wrong idea, she was not the least bit mean or short with me. It was as if she just saw me as this normal ordinary guy, which I desperately wanted a woman to see in me. So when she approached me that night, there was no insecurity. She was confident and convinced of who she was in Christ.

I hope that you will pay attention to this chapter because if you are like me, you struggle with insecurity. I bet you have compared yourself to other people and found yourself feeling like the loser. You may even lie in bed at night dreaming about what it would be like if you could make people laugh or be the life of the party or lose twenty-five pounds or be working a better job or get that hot girl to talk to you.

I think the reason we struggle so much with insecurity is not that we have no security. I think we just have security in the wrong things.

As a Christian, your security should be in Jesus Christ and what He accomplished for you on the cross. Our identity is in Him. We are His. He owns us. We are valuable because He assigned value to us. We are special because He created us. We have meaning because He loves us.

It is one thing to say this, but it is another thing to live like you believe it. Few Christians can honestly say that they are completely secure in Christ. Unfortunately we find our security elsewhere.

A person who shows extreme signs of insecurity should make you stop and think long and hard about a long-term relationship and what that might mean.

Here are some of the places we find our security other than Christ.
Popularity
Money
Athletic Ability
Education
Family
Body shape and size
Academic Achievement
And last but not least...WHO WE DATE

I am absolutely certain that most of the teenagers I meet who are dating someone are not dating because they are seriously hoping to marry soon. They are just dating them because it is social suicide to be single and not hooking up with someone. You know it's true! People treat you like you are weird if you don't date. They wonder what is wrong with you if you don't flirt or surround yourself with dating drama. It is the rite of passage into the elusive world of teenage cool.

I am also convinced that cliques form with people who share the same insecurities. We assume that they form among those of similar fashion, style, economic background, and common interests. And while these are true, I believe that one of the underlying factors in the formation of our exclusive clubs and cliques is that certain people who are insecure about the same thing end up gravitating toward each other.

For instance, a clique of foul-mouthed jocks at your high school who perhaps put down geeks or nerds and treat girls with disrespect would most likely share an insecurity about their intelligence (thus making fun of the nerds) and about their ability to have a serious relationship (thus making fun of females).

A clique of technical geniuses who love video games and computers may stand in judgment of athletes, calling them names like idiots, blockheads, dumb jocks, or illiterate (I have heard all of these used). There is a great chance that those in the clique share a common insecurity about the thing they make fun of; in this situation perhaps they are jealous of the abilities of the student athletes they chide and jeer. Do they wish they could run faster or jump higher or play sports in front of hundreds of fans while they cheer for them?

A clique of well-dressed, good-looking girls sits together in the cafeteria every single day and point and laugh at people. They make fun of what other girls are wearing. They say that certain girls are fat or ugly. Maybe they talk about certain couples and why they should not be together. Every girl at that table most likely has an insecurity about themselves; their weight, their hair, their lack of a boyfriend, or their popularity.

This may seem like a broad generalization, but if you have ever paid attention, you know how mean and ugly people in groups can be to others. I can remember it all the way back to kindergarten when a group of about four of us (myself included) made fun of a little girl for wearing "ugly cowboy boots." Of course children are going to do that, and even as adults, we must learn to ignore people who criticize us as a result of their own insecurities. However, if you notice these things in a person you are interested in dating or marrying, red flags should begin to fly!

Obviously, the reason why people lash out, make fun, and verbally hurt others is to cover up their own insecurities, but that is not to say that everyone who is insecure is mean. And here is the balance on this issue; you will never meet someone who is totally secure. In the same way, you will never be totally secure as a person. We are just not perfect (though many of you married men reading this would say, quite seriously, that your wife is pretty close!). In other words, you will probably end up spending the rest of your life with someone who struggles, just like you, with insecurities.

The red flags here should come when you begin to wonder if this person you are attracted to or dating has serious issues in this area that affect everyone they come in contact with.

Consider some of the following questions.
Have you noticed that he tends to put on a sad face and pout for no apparent reason?

When you ask her what is wrong, is she unable to tell you anything at all?

Do you end up playing a guessing game about why she is mad with you, refusing to ever really share anything concrete?

Is there constant jealousy when you spend time with your friends or family?

Are you made to feel guilty for not spending enough time with this person?

Does he dig up past arguments and throw them back in your face whenever you have a disagreement?

Is she unwilling to forgive you when you ask her to?

Is he critical of others, especially those who are well liked and popular?

Is she jealous of other people's success?

Does he find fault with beautiful and attractive people?

Is she moody?

Do you have to walk on eggshells around him for fear that you could "set him off" about something?

As you ask these questions, you will need to discern for yourself if he or she is just struggling with normal everyday issues or if he or she is has a serious problem with insecurity, because someone who is defined by their jealousy, cynicism, and criticism of others will eventually turn those same things on you.

Insecure people are able to maintain relationships by manipulation. I dated a girl like that once for a few weeks in high school, and I began to notice that her demeanor would change. She would put on a sad face every time we talked. If it was on the phone, she would either talk like a pouty baby, or she would just give me the silent treatment. She wanted me to beg her to tell me what was wrong. Then she would refuse to tell me. When I got frustrated and gave up, she would tell me that I did not love her. After about three weeks of this nonsense, I told her one night on the phone, "You are right. I don't!" and that was the end of it.

I would suggest that some of you do the same. Healthy relationships and Godly marriages are not built on manipulation and insecurity. They are instead based upon honesty and open communication. If you think it is difficult dating someone who is insecure, you should try marrying someone like that! Actually, don't do that.

Maybe one of the reasons so many student relationships follow this pattern is because most teenagers are more insecure than they are confident in themselves. That is not a bad thing! I was like that, and most students are because they are developing their identity and their character. So let this be a warning to you. It is probably better for you, if you are a teenager or even a young college student, to go slowly in relationships. Do not make dating your goal. Make holiness and obedience your goal. When you go out, do it in groups. And as you develop your identity and character, you will become more secure in Jesus and one day you will be ready for a lifetime of love with a mate that will not manipulate you into staying around. That is the kind of marriage I have, and I have no regrets!

Chapter 25
Lack of Self-Control, Short Fuse, & Laziness

Similarly, encourage the young men to be self-controlled.
Titus 2:6 (NIV)

Therefore, prepare your minds for action; be self-controlled; set your hope full on the grace to be given you when Jesus Christ is revealed. I Peter 1:13 (NIV)

How many times have you seen this scenario unfold: A guy and a girl at school, the park, a restaurant, or any old public place are obviously "together." As they talk, you notice that her facial expression is sour, scared, or frustrated. His voice sounds angry, impatient, and irritated. They are obviously in a disagreement about something, who knows what. It begins to escalate. You cannot help but eavesdrop, I mean that is what humans do (maybe the same part of us that makes us want to slow down at a wreck or watch a fight in middle school between two of our classmates). Before long, the guy has erupted. He slings verbal abuse her way. He calls her names. He reminds her how good he has been to her. He points at her and tightens every muscle in his face and neck. Veins bulge. Vocal chords stretch. She looks embarrassed and afraid. She begins to cry. The more she sobs the angrier he gets. He has blown a fuse, and everyone within earshot knows it.

What just happened? If you have been out of the house to a public place, whether it be a ball-game or Wal-Mart, you have probably witnessed something similar to this. You may even be thinking "He just described me when I get upset!" This familiar scene is the result of one of our little "red flags" and it is simply a lack of self-control.

A lack of self-control can manifest itself in multiple ways, and if you are in a relationship with someone or are considering it and you see a few of these rear their ugly heads, take a step back and consider if you want to be with someone who may have a fundamental character flaw in the area of self-control.

Tendency to over-indulge in entertainment
Watches hours of TV daily
Binges on food when stressed, angry or upset
Has a serious problem overeating
Addicted to fad diets or exercise routines that never last long
Spends enormous amounts of money on personal pleasure or
*   entertainment*
Frequently yells, screams, or gets angry with others
Quickly changes moods from good to bad when something
*   unplanned happens*

Oversleeps regularly
Runs late most of the time for appointments, school, friends, etc.
Is always broke and borrowing money from people; a "moocher"
Plays hours of video games without stopping
Cannot keep a job for more than a few weeks
Never dates someone for very long
Complains about work or chores all the time
Expects others to always do everything for them
Blames others when they mess up or drop the ball
Is extremely messy and unorganized with no desire to change
Generally lacks discipline in all areas of life
Has an addiction (food, drugs, cutting, drinking, shopping,
*   pornography, etc.)*
Can't handle adversity or change without a major blow-up

It would be easy to point out a select few examples, and we will do just that. The main concern, however, is that you be warned about a greater and more general issue than just a few areas of slackness. For sure, every teenager and young adult struggles with the normal stages of development and it is unrealistic to expect a sixteen year old or even a recent college graduate to behave with the same level of responsibility that a forty year-old attorney or teacher would possess. I am not elevating an unattainable standard here. What I am encouraging, however, is critical thinking on your part when it comes to the kind of person you want to marry. The goal is marriage for life. If that is the case, then you need to know if a potential lifetime mate has serious issues with self-control.

Let's face it. Self-control is the absolute last thing that you will be encouraged to develop as an American. We are encouraged in the opposite direction. We are told to go for it. Fast food restaurants tell you "Have it your way." If someone wants to share your snack, potato chip companies tell them "Get your own bag!" Just recently, I was told at a drive-through window that I could super size my value meal and get an extra gallon of Sprite and the Extreme-Economy-Giant-Fries for only forty-nine cents. What a deal!

According to <u>National Geographic</u>, the average American is subject to ten hours of media stimulation a day. This includes TV, radio, billboards, and every imaginable medium possible. The average American watches five hours of TV a day (I am proudly not a member of that group). And at every crook and turn, you are told that you deserve bigger, better, and more everything!

We are, generally speaking, a lazy, consumer-minded, materialistic culture who wants what we want when we want it and if we don't get it we gripe loud enough until we get someone's attention who can get it for us. You don't believe me? Spend a spattering of time doing the research.

Here are a few scary facts that I hope you will consider.

One of every three Americans is obese (31%)
Two in three Americans is overweight (59%)
The average American will witness 16,000 acts of TV violence by
*   age eighteen*
One of every two new marriages in America ends in divorce
America has 7% of the world's population
America consumes 25% the world's natural resources
And this one is the scariest of all...By 2005, obesity will replace smoking as
*   the number one killer in America, killing more people than alcoholism,*
*   drug abuse, murder, and automobile accidents.*

We cannot stick with what we start. We are addicted to fad diets and overnight fix-it-all solutions. We would rather take a pill that has not even been FDA tested than discipline ourselves to eat less and exercise more. One foray into late-night TV and you will be convinced of our insatiable desire for the shortcut; infomercials promise happiness with everything from a Bow-flex to colon-blow laxatives. Will this ever stop?

I need not continue. Suffice it to say, our culture, if you listen, will teach you to be a self-serving, apathetic, addicted, undisciplined human being. We will have to fight tooth and nail as Christians to live counter to our culture, practicing the virtues found in scripture and striving to live for Jesus Christ. With this continual onslaught of advertising and self-centeredness, is it possible to find someone who goes against the grain? Is there any hope to find that special girl or guy who understands sacrifice and selflessness? You bet there is!

The first step, however, is becoming aware of your own tendencies towards a lack of discipline or self-control. Get to work on those things now, because marriage has enough challenges of its own without trying to grow up after you have tied the knot. Your spouse is not a surrogate mama or daddy and their job is not to raise you. You should be sufficiently raised and mature when you walk the aisle. If that bothers you, perhaps you may want to back up a step and work on your own spiritual growth before you embark on a potential marriage relationship. (How many times have I said that already in this book?)

I said that there was hope in finding someone with good habits of discipline and self-control. The first step is to NEVER SETTLE FOR LESS. Don't lower your standards because you are desperate or lonely. If someone can't make the cut, then they get cut. Wait, no matter how long it takes, until you meet someone that meets your expectations and God's expectations for you. One of my closest friends and fellow minister of the gospel was not married until he was forty years old. He did not settle for less and now has a beautiful wife and two great kids. When my family goes to visit them in Bryson City, NC, we have wonderful times of fellowship together. He could have married the first woman who was looking to have a baby before her biological clock ticked out, but he waited on God's best for him. Wait on God as long as it takes.

The next step is to quit saying that there are no good guys or girls out there. I get so tired of this! "There just aren't any good girls here in this town" or, "Where are all the good Christian guys? They're not here on this campus?" I think these comments show where the real problem lies; our vision is way too limited. Just because your little town with two red lights has not yet produced for you a dashing young man with a nice bank account, blue eyes, and unquestionable Godly character does not mean that the whole planet is void of such a man! Have you actually been to every town, city, village, and college on earth and checked to make sure that the last mature, disciplined, Christian guy has just been taken off the market? Quit looking at only what you can see and start looking to Christ to be your satisfaction. As you pray for your mate, God is orchestrating all sorts of strange and unpredictable circumstances to bring you and that person together when you are ready. Quit fretting. And quit settling!

Ask anyone who has been married for more than twenty years, and you will get a rude awakening. It gets harder and harder to change as we get older, and as a Christian you know the only way to change is by the Holy Spirit. So quit trying to date these people who have no discipline and change them on your own. You cannot change them! Unless of course you are the Holy Spirit, which I doubt you are.

If after reading this chapter you realize that you lack self-control and carry the characteristics of a lazy and undisciplined person, instead of diving into a relationship that you will quickly and surely ruin, invest the time you might normally waste on entertainment or TV by getting serious about growing in Christ. You are not ready for someone, except for Jesus. Don't hurt them and yourself. Wait.

If you sense the person you like embodies many of these characteristics, pay attention to the red flags. Do not talk yourself into staying in a relationship with a baby that won't change. Get out and focus on whom Jesus is and who you are in Christ. The big day will come soon enough, and you don't want to face that day with regret.

Chapter 26

Addiction To Drama & Moodiness

For we hear that some among you are leading an undisciplined life,
doing no work at all, but acting like busybodies.
2 Thessalonians 3:11 (NASB)

Drama! Many folks despise it, some people love it, and others just can't seem to live without it! Come on, you know the type of person I'm talking about. They aren't happy if there's not some catastrophe brewing. If somebody's not saying something nasty about somebody else, these people don't know what to do with themselves. Our key verse describes this person well: an undisciplined, unfocused busybody! My middle and high school days were often filled with drama. Pointless, time wasting, good for nothing drama. Boyfriend/girlfriend, he said she said, will someone please stop the madness kind of drama. I beckon you to fly far away from the universe of drama. I plead with you to step down from your throne where you currently reign as the drama queen of your world. And I warn you that if you are addicted to drama, or your relationship creates constant drama, you're in big trouble.

Granted, as a student you're dealing with a ton of fluctuating emotions. And it can be difficult to make sense of everything that's going on in your life, especially in the arena of love. I don't want to make light of the situations that cause you to get worked up, or say that it doesn't truly matter, because it matters a lot. The feelings you have in your heart are real and valid, and I totally respect them. However, God never intended for you to live in the state of moodiness and inconsistency that drama creates. There is more to life than running around spreading the latest gossip or crying your eyes out because you just broke up with your third boyfriend this month. Drama distracts you from the true purposes of God. Drama disables you from having an effective ministry to those around you. How can you minister to anyone else when your life is an emotional mess?

How do you know if you're addicted to drama? Let me ask a few diagnostic questions. If you answer yes to several of these, we've got some work to do.

Have you been in "serious" dating relationships with several people in the
*   last year?*
Do you act like you're married when you date someone? This would
*   include things like talking about marriage in the infant stages of a*
*   dating relationship, long before it's appropriate.*
Do you always find yourself in the middle of somebody else's business?
Do you feel incomplete unless you're dating somebody, or at least in
*   the process of hooking up with somebody?*

*Are you forever "pouring out your heart" to your friends, crying and
freaking out about something or somebody?
Are you the one who always has the latest gossip?
Are you the one who's always on a mission to learn the latest gossip?
Do you spend hours and hours on the phone or internet counseling or
being counseled about the latest dating crisis?
Do you act like the world is coming to an end when even the
smallest thing doesn't go your way?
Is your attitude and outlook on life like a roller-coaster? Do you have
drastic mood swings?*

After you've asked these questions of yourself, I strongly urge you to
evaluate anybody you consider dating using these questions. I don't care how
pretty a girl is, if she is addicted to drama, she will suck the life out of you, fellas.
Ladies, I don't care how sensitive or sweet a guy is, if he is a melodramatic
emotional time bomb, you need to remain "just friends" and let him grow up.

The addiction to drama that is so prevalent during middle school and
high school is one of the reasons I strongly believe that most of you aren't ready
to date anyone yet. Dating requires an enormous amount of emotional and
physical maturity. When fourteen and fifteen year-olds try to have an exclusive
relationship with a person of the opposite sex, and their emotional foundation is
not yet solid, all manner of confusion and mistakes is sure to follow. When two
people date prematurely, the emotional problems of each individual are
multiplied and magnified. Rather than curing the addiction to drama with a
deep, satisfying relationship with Christ, those who date too early look for
fulfillment and satisfaction in each other. Since only God can fulfill the hunger
for Himself that He has instilled in every human being, when two people look to
each other to have this hunger pacified, both people end up extremely
disappointed. So the natural result is drama. Couples argue, break up, get back
together, date each other's friends, do the hokey poky and turn themselves
around, and permanent emotional scars are the result.

Another problem with constant drama is the poor witness that it is to
unbelievers. If you, as a Christian, aren't full enough of the Holy Spirit to have
the wisdom and discernment to skip the drama, why would your unsaved friends
want to serve your God? Do you want to win your friends to Christ? Let them
see the emotional stability that Christ has provided for you. Let them see that
your identity isn't wrapped up in who you're dating. Let them observe your focus
on the glory of God, and let that focus guard you from the drama Olympics in
which most students involve themselves.

One of the most attractive things about my wife is her level headed,
even keel approach to life. She is the same person from one day to the next, and
she's not spasmodic in her commitment to me. She's solid emotionally, and that
makes our life so much easier. Okay, so she has some bad days, and she cries

sometimes when she's stressed out. She cries sometimes for no apparent reason (It's a girl thing!), and that's okay too. Because at the core of who she is there is great consistency and a solid value system which guides all of her decisions. Her identity is in Christ, not in her circumstances. Perhaps the greatest thing that attracted me to Holly initially was that she wasn't even looking for anybody to date. She was content, secure, and steady in Christ, and far removed from the emotional drama of the average college freshman's mad quest for love.

You have been granted the right to live above the drama. The blood of Christ purchased your salvation and secured your identity. Refuse to live in the realm of the melodramatic. Choose to spend your time and emotional energies on lasting things. Pour yourself into the work of God, which has eternal rewards. If you're in a relationship built on drama, or if you're a drama fest waiting to happen, back out of the dating scene and get back to the basics of knowing Christ and making Him known. And once and for all, STOP THE DRAMA!

Chapter 27
Incompatability

Do two walk together unless they have agreed to do so?
Amos 3:3 (NIV)

One area that some people never even consider when preparing for marriage is the most obvious area that needs attention; are we even compatible? Can we get along with each other for forty or fifty years? This may seem like a rather selfish question to ask. If marriage is about serving my mate, then why should I even entertain the question of compatibility? So what if we are totally different? Love conquers all!

Oh, the blindness of youth and idealism...I am not talking about marrying someone who is exactly the same as you. That would be suicide and you would kill each other, too. I am talking about marrying someone who is compatible with you.

Someone you can share a bathroom with.
Someone who is willing to change.
Someone who is patient.
Someone who is flexible.
Someone who can adjust to the stresses and challenges of life.
Someone who shares your desire for children, or lack thereof.
Someone you trust wholeheartedly without reservation.
Someone you want to grow old with.
Someone who has a heart to serve God and you, as well.
Someone who is not high-maintenance, addicted to drama and demanding.
Someone who is willing to try new things.
Someone who can open up and share how they feel.
Someone who won't hold grudges against you.
Someone who shares your convictions about life and faith in Christ.

This list is not exhaustive, but may be a good place to start for you. Some people were simply not meant to marry each other, and if you can avoid marrying someone like that, then you and they are better off. Don't be deceived into thinking that all those little differences and issues will just work themselves out. In marriage, NOTHING works itself out. NOTHING! Things are fixed when both people are willing to humble themselves, listen, and change things that need changing.

Like me, you have heard that opposites attract. This is true in many cases, but that attraction can quickly turn around on you, for as Max Lucado says, "After marriage, opposites attack!" This is not to say that two different people are doomed when they unite in marriage. Rather, it means that some of those little quirks and habits that you thought were so cute about the other person when you were dating easily grate on your nerves and drive you crazy after a few years in the same house. (Note: If you are married and looking for a justification to be upset with your spouse over something, you can't use this as your excuse. You have made the covenant of marriage, so get in there and work it out like a mature adult).

One of the most important things for me when I was single was making sure that I never got involved with a girl who did not feel the same call into ministry as me. I knew that I would have to marry a special kind of girl; one who had a common goal and purpose in life. She would have to have the same desire for ministry as me. She could not have expensive tastes or a materialistic streak. She would need to love people and traveling and all that goes along with being a minister and being married to a minister. I met numerous Godly and attractive girls in college and after graduation. I had strong feelings for a few of them, too. But the conversation would always come to a snag. We would have "the talk." I would tell them about my call into the ministry and where I saw the rest of my life heading and the sacrifices and challenges of life in ministry. As I described what my wife would have to be willing to endure, their faces would get longer and their eyes sadder and sadder.

It was tough watching this happen time and time again, especially when it was a girl I really liked. In the long run, however, I see the Lord's wisdom in the whole process. Not only was I protected from marrying a girl who wanted something totally different out of life, but think about how blessed those poor girls were! Can you imaging how miserable they would have been marrying me! Traveling 200 days a year, multiple trips to India and the Himalayas, the never-ending grind of the ministry! (I don't want to make it sound like there were thirty girls I had this talk with, it was more like three or four).

By asking these kinds of questions, you will be wiser and happier in the future. You may be saying, "I am still young and I have no idea what I want to do with my life, so how can I ask these questions?" You are right. There are a few exceptional cases where a teenager or college student has a clear sense of call and destiny, and they know where they are going. The vast majority of us sort of "hunt and peck" the future. We take it as it comes and learn from our mistakes as we make them. This does not mean, though, that you can't ask anything at all.

For instance, start by asking if you are compatible in the area of your faith. If the person is not even a Christian, then run away immediately. I will say it loud and clear, it is NOT God's will for you to DATE or MARRY an unbeliever.

Do not be unequally yoked with an unbeliever, for what do righteousness and wickedness have in common? Or what fellowship can light have with darkness? 2 Corinthians 6:14 (NIV)

Now I know that some say they are dating people to lead them to Jesus, and since we have already dealt with this silly argument in previous chapters, I will refer you back there for a thorough and logical explanation of why Christianity is incompatible with other religions in marriage.

What if you were raised wealthy, and you are an only child who is used to having nice things? There is nothing wrong with having nice things, but can your boyfriend who was raised dirt-poor in a family of five make you happy? Unless you break away and change from your upbringing, he will most likely not be able to give you the things that you have always been used to having. To be fair, you are not doomed to live out your childhood. Thousands of marriages between people like this work, and praise God for them. But are you sure you want to take that risk?

Is your heart set on being a doctor? Great! You realize you will be in school ten to twelve years for that. Does your boyfriend, who feels called to be a missionary, feel ok with waiting that long? Have you guys even had that talk yet?

In preparation for this chapter, my mind was flooded with so many sad stories of friends of mine who were bitten by the love bug and threw reason out the door. One case immediately comes to mind.

A college buddy had met a young lady who had just finished high school. He burst into my dorm room late one evening after one of their first dates. "She is THE ONE. I know it, Clayton. I am gonna marry that girl!" I listened patiently and offered little advice, hoping that some of the emotion would calm after a few weeks. Instead, after a few weeks they had already decided to get married. They had planned to wait two years, then one year, and then six months. A small group of us tried to reason with him, but to no avail. I asked him to wait longer. I told him she was too young and immature to get married. I told him that he was too young and immature to get married. Neither had a job, and he had student loans. But most importantly, he had surrendered his life to the ministry, to preach and to be worship leader. She, on the other hand, had told him that she did not see herself as a minister or a minister's wife.

He told me this, and when I reminded him of her words, he explained his plan to change things once they were married. "Once she sees how awesome ministry is and how much fun it is to travel and see people come to Christ, she will be hooked and unable to stay away from it. Plus, I am praying everyday that God would change her heart and that she would have a desire to be my partner in ministry."

I all but begged him to reconsider. I asked him to just wait another six months, but he said it was God's will that they not wait. I said it would still be God's will in six more months, but it was as useless as talking to a stop sign. His mind was made up.

Fast-forward now with me. The wedding is over. The honeymoon is a distant memory. The house is a mess and the bills have piled up. He has quit college, and she can't get a job that pays more than $6 an hour with her education. He never finished college and she never started. Within a year, they are both ready for a divorce. She feels unfulfilled living with a man who is seldom home, and he resents the fact that she won't minister with him. She wants a bigger house and a pool and new car. He just wants to keep the power turned on at the house. So she decides to venture out one day on the advice of a friend. She meets an "employer" who says she can make $300 a night. She becomes an "exotic dancer" and falls in love with her boss. She leaves home with a simple note left on the fridge. I saw the note and read these very words;

"I am so sorry. I just could not do it anymore. I am not happy with you and I hate this place. You are always out preaching, and I am just not cut out for this Christian stuff. I will come by sometime when you are gone and get the rest of my stuff. I am so sorry, at least we didn't have children."

Could this happen to you? It certainly could, and it does, every single day to thousands of Americans who never stop to ask simple little important questions that, when answered honestly, can spare them a lifetime of regret.

Do you want a marriage without regret? Then pay attention to the little things before you get to the altar. It may hurt, but you are better off not even getting emotionally involved with someone you are totally incompatible with. Remember, you will be living with this person for the rest of your life. Just because you have feelings of love and attraction for them does not mean that it is God's will for you to marry them.

You were raised out in the country, and you hate traffic and the big city. You like fresh air and a fireplace, and you wave at everyone you meet. Your girlfriend was raised in Atlanta and was terrified the first time you waved at a stranger, telling you that you could get shot doing that where she came from. You love simple things like fishing and hunting and tractors. She likes musicals, broadway, and getting dressed up. She loves to paint and you love to watch <u>The Dukes of Hazard</u>. She cleans all the time and you are sloppy and messy. Are you sure the two of you can get along? Will you be able to compromise? Where will you live? Can it work?

Sure it can! Charie and I are living proof, and the above paragraph proves it. But it took hard work and lots of talking to get to the point where we knew, no matter what happens, we would stick together and love each other despite our differences. We were different, but not incompatible.

I pray for you, that when you begin to see the differences in you and the person you want to be with, that you will have the courage and the grace to talk about those differences. Be brave enough to work through them if you choose to, but be bold enough to walk away if the differences are too great and make you an incompatible pair.

Chapter 28

Lack Of Respect For Parents & Authority

Honor your father and your mother, that your days may be prolonged in the land which the LORD your God gives you.
Exodus 20:12 (NASB)

Ladies, do you want to know how to see into the future? Would you like to look ahead twenty years and see how the guy you're currently interested in would treat you if you were his wife? I'll tell you how to do it: watch the way he treats his mom. Guys have a wonderful way of being sweet, thoughtful, and considerate during the beginning phases of relationship. A guy can be awfully impressive while he's trying to win your heart, but if what you're after is a lasting love, you need to look beyond whether he sends you roses or refrains from burping during meals, and figure out exactly what kind of character he possesses. I can think of no better way to observe true character than to evaluate the way an individual treats his or her parents. And until you've learned how to honor your parents, you're not ready to take on the responsibility of honoring any other human being in a romantic relationship.

Our key scripture is a familiar one-it is the fifth of the ten commandments, and obedience to this commandment is desperately needed in our society. I am constantly appalled by the lack of respect for authority-especially parents-that I witness in this "say what you feel/nobody can tell you what to do" culture. Recently, I was in an airport in Greensboro, NC, and I overheard the most disturbing dialogue between two teenage girls and their mother. (You never know who's listening...be careful how you talk to your mother or you might end up being a preacher's example in his book on dating!) I didn't intend to eavesdrop, but the girls were so loud I couldn't help but hear every word they said. I didn't take notes, but the disrespectful attitude they had toward their mother made such an impression on me that I still remember several of the things they said. These are direct quotes:

> *"God, Mom, you're so stupid!"*
> *"Mom, are you a freakin' idiot?"*
> *"Shut up Mom, I'll do whatever I want."*
> *"I'll get a dog if I want to get a dog, and you'll pay for it."*
> *"Mom, I swear, you get on my nerves so bad!"*
> *"I can't stand you, you're embarrassing me!"*

I sat and listened, stunned by their ability to talk this way to the woman who brought them into the world. I should have turned around, looked those girls in the eye, and preached a little sermon for them. Or maybe I should have smacked them. Then I could have called Holly to come to the Greensboro prison facility with plenty of bail money.

If you talk to your mother or father this way, you desperately need God's convicting and changing power. It is a terrible offense to God.

"But what if my parents are unfair to me?"
"Do I still have to honor them?"
Yes.
"My parents split up a long time ago."
"I can't respect them."
I understand what you're thinking, but you still must honor them.
"I'll honor my parents when they start respecting me."
It doesn't work that way.

The reason I can answer these objections with such confidence is that no matter how poorly your parents may be performing and regardless of the way they treat you, they are your God ordained parents. So to dishonor them is to dishonor God, plain and simple. In fact, this principle applies to any authority figure in your life. Romans 13:1-2 states: "For there is no authority except from God, and those which exist are established by God. Therefore whoever resists authority has opposed the ordinance of God; and they who have opposed will receive condemnation upon themselves." Whether you like them or not, whether you agree with them or not, you must honor your authorities. When you do this, you honor God, and God will honor your obedience.

Many of you have good parents. Of course they aren't perfect, but they're doing the best they can. It should be even more natural for you to appreciate them, obey them, and submit to them. However, we often think we know everything during our growing up years. I recently heard an older man joke, "The older I get, the smarter my parents become." One day you'll understand (gosh I sound like my parents! But it's true...) that your parents usually know what's best. God gave them to you for protection.

Do you want to practice being a good husband or wife? The dating scene isn't the best practice field...your home is. Guys, open the door for your mother when she is walking into a building. Ladies, accept your Dad's position as the spiritual leader of your house, and follow him as he follows Christ. If he doesn't follow Christ, love him and serve him until he does. But do not under any circumstances make excuses for yourself to live in disobedience to your parents. The way you treat your parents is a direct reflection of the way you feel about God. If Jesus has a high place in your life, you'll cherish and love your family. If Jesus is just a casual part of your existence, you'll take your parents for granted and suffer the consequences.

If I had ever talked to my mother the way those girls in the airport spoke to their mother that day, I know exactly what she would have done. In fact, she did it once. As a little boy I once made the fatal mistake of telling my mom to shut up. She didn't say a word. She got up from the table, walked into the bathroom, turned on the sink and called my name. I started to shake, and for a moment I tried to decide whether to run, hide under the table, or beg for mercy. I decided to take what I had coming to me, so I walked into the bathroom, not knowing what to expect. My 5'4" mother had a bar of soap in her hand, and a look that said, "You'll never tell me to shut up again" on her face. She inserted the bar of soap into my mouth and literally washed out my mouth with soap, something she never had to do again. I can still taste the soap in my mouth as I write and reflect on this traumatically wonderful experience. Parents, please demand that your kids honor you, whether you use a bar of soap, a yardstick or an intricate reward or consequence system. It is God's established order! They need to know who's in charge! Students, when you do not honor your parents, you are removing yourself from their protection and rebelling against God Himself.

If you are considering dating a girl who gets a serious attitude when her mother tells her she can't leave the house wearing a certain outfit, watch out! This girl has a problem with authority, and it will show up in every area of her life. If you are dating a young man who is always mouthing off at teachers or coaches, he will one day abuse you with that same mouth, young lady! Get out while you can. And if you want to learn to be the perfect husband, start where you live. Your parents have a lot to offer, and you have a lot to learn!

Chapter 29

A Wild Tongue & Gossip

The wise in heart are called discerning, and pleasant words promote instruction. Proverbs 16:21 (NIV)

The tongue has the power of life and death, and those who love it will eat its fruit. Proverbs 18:21 (NIV)

Have you ever been witness to someone else's embarrassment? I am not talking about someone tripping and falling off the sidewalk or dropping an ice cream cone on a child or an old lady's head. What I am speaking of is brutal, faces turn red, you want to "crawl in a hole" kind of embarrassment for someone!

Several years ago I was in a restaurant with a large crowd of folks from a local church I had just finished preaching in. The food had arrived and we gave thanks. When we began eating, the pastor's wife said to her husband "No wonder you are forty pounds overweight! Look at all that food. If you eat like that, you are going to keep on looking like a hippo." Then she just died laughing, as if she could cover up her insensitivity with a chuckle.

She had a big mouth. Really big. I was single at the time and promised myself that I would never ever in a thousand years marry a woman who had loose lips like that, even if she were the last woman in the infinite cosmos.

It is one thing to mess around with your close friends in a playful and fun manner. I do that with my friends. And a little bit of picking is fine within a marriage as long as it is done with care and caution, never crossing the line where it hurts feelings. Charie and I do that all the time, but we can both tell by just looking at each other if we have gone too far.

Here is a red flag for you to begin thinking about right now; do you have a big mouth? Do you gossip about people? What about the person you are dating or considering a relationship with?

The scriptures are full of warnings about people who can't control their tongue, and at every place in the Bible where this is brought up, we are warned to do several things with those kinds of people; avoid them, ignore them, rebuke them, don't talk to them, or run away from them. Just take a few minutes one day and check your Bible concordance for words like gossip, tongue, mouth, or slander. Look up the verses pertaining to these words, and you will be amazed at how serious God takes this issue. If it is such a big deal to God, then shouldn't we pay attention to our own sin of gossip and also to how other people use their mouths?

Why does God place so much importance on the power of the tongue? When we grew up, we always sang, "Sticks and stones will break my bones but names will never hurt me." Now that I am a bit older, I realize that whoever wrote that was either really dumb or had never been called a name. If someone says something mean about you, no matter how much he or she may have been joking or how tough you try to be, it hurts. God knows how devastating evil words and slanderous gossip can be to his children. Much like I want to protect and defend my wife if someone slanders her or hurts her with careless words, Christ wants to protect his bride, the church (all of his children) from the painful effects of careless words. He is a jealous God, and that is not a bad thing in the way that we think of jealousy. I am jealous of my wife and am unwilling to share her with another man. In the same way, God is jealous and protective of his children and does not want their lives ruined by people who can't control their tongue.

Be careful when you notice someone joking in a harsh way with people, and think about this verse that clearly deals with this issue.

Like a madman shooting firebrands or deadly arrows is a man who deceives his neighbor and says "I was only joking". Proverbs 26:18-19 (NIV)

Do you see how dangerous it is to become close or intimate with someone who is hurtful with his words? You can never trust him. You don't know if he is kidding or if he is serious. How do you know if he joking around when he tells you how he feels about you? It is thin ice to tread on, and you had better be ready to fall if you date someone who practices this kind of humor. If you do this, be aware of how your idea of fun can devastate someone's identity or self-esteem. I still remember a guy on my basketball team making fun of my white legs in the 6th grade. For years I was self-conscious about it. (Actually, if he had been looking closely he would have realized that my legs are a few shades lighter than white, actually classified as "glow-in-the-dark"). Do not ever think that you can just throw the words, "I was joking" or, "Just kidding" at the end of a sentence and that will make everything ok.

Do you want to be in a relationship with someone who is constantly talking bad about people behind their backs? Here is a promise that you can take to the bank: if they talk about others behind their back, they will do the same to you. It is a character issue. If they are not trustworthy to keep their mouth shut concerning other people, then they will not have the character to keep a secret that you have shared with them. If they betray the confidence of one person, what makes anyone else any different; they will betray your confidence as well. If you find yourself feeling unsure or uneasy about sharing intimate or personal things with your boyfriend or girlfriend because you feel like you can't trust him or her, it is due to one thing. You can't! Pay attention to your first impression. Many times that is how God gives us discernment in situations. So don't ignore those uneasy feelings.

You can also tell a good deal about how wild a person's tongue is by what others have to say about him and his "gossip habits." Make sure that you understand that this is not a license to believe any rumor that you hear about someone. We have already established that the right thing to do is to approach someone if you have heard things about him and see if they are true or not. Of course you can't do this with every situation or you would be spending your whole life confronting people. But when it comes to a person you may be interested in dating or marrying, pay attention to what others say about him, especially if he has a reputation of using his mouth to slander, deceive, lie, or hurt. Then approach him in humility and ask him about it, making a wise and discerning choice about where the relationship should go from there.

One more thing needs to be mentioned in regards to how we use our words to affect others. Make sure you notice, in your own life and in the life of the person you are interested it, how quickly she speaks. Here is what I mean; does she (or you) have a bad habit of saying whatever is on her mind at the moment without any thought of how appropriate those words are? Does she fail to consider how her words may hurt feelings or make a situation uncomfortable? It is simply inconceivable to think that we can just spout off exactly what we think without any worry of repercussion or negative results. If a politician says one word incorrectly, he or she can suffer embarrassment for years to come. The same is true with ministers, and not just regarding the pulpit! I have to hold my tongue often times when I would love to spew forth a few paragraphs straight from the heart, telling people what I really think. However, we can't live and thrive in a civilized and educated culture saying whatever comes to mind. It is social suicide.

Therefore, it is imperative that you listen closely to yourself and your love interest. If he regularly blurts out immature or ignorant words at inopportune times, causing embarrassment to those around him, that is a red flag. If he doesn't have the discernment to understand certain social situations and seems to even enjoy the controversy he creates by saying inappropriate things, then that is a red flag. If he does not know how to hold his tongue, it is a sign of a greater issue and a deeper immaturity.

Even a fool is thought wise if he keeps silent, and discerning if he holds his tongue. Proverbs 17:28 (NIV)

This verse exemplifies the characteristic you should possess and that you should look for in a mate. It reveals wisdom when one is able to read a given situation and hold back words that could be misunderstood or misquoted. I have learned to keep quiet in important meetings with lots of people present until I am asked to speak. Usually the first person to verbalize their opinion is forgotten by the end of the meeting, but the person who waits to be called upon at the end of the matter often times has the "last word" on the issue, and that last word is the one that lingers in the mind and ears of the hearer. Just be cautious of someone with a wild tongue and a big mouth, and if you see that you struggle with this, ask the Lord to give you strength to hold back. Ask for wisdom to know when to speak and when to listen. Ask for discernment to know when you should not say anything at all or when to speak a kind word that can diffuse a tense situation.

I can't think of a better way to end this chapter than to allow you to read these words straight from the scriptures about the power of the tongue; more powerful than dynamite, more destructive than an atomic bomb, more hurtful than a poisonous snake. Watch out for this red flag in others, but most importantly in yourself.

When we put bits into the mouths of horses to make them obey us, we can turn the whole animal. Or take ships as an example. Although they are so large and are driven by strong winds, they are steered by a very small rudder wherever the pilot wants to go. Likewise the tongue is a small part of the body, but it makes great boasts. Consider what a great forest is set on fire by a small spark. The tongue is also a fire, a world of evil among the parts of the body. It corrupts the whole person, sets the whole course of his life on fire, and is itself set on fire by hell. All kinds of animals, birds, and reptiles and creatures of the sea are being tamed and have been tamed by man, but no man can tame the tongue. It is a restless evil, full of deadly poison. James 3:3-8 (NIV)

Chapter 30

Without Excuse

Suppose one of you wants to build a tower. Will he not first sit down and estimate the cost to see if he has enough money to complete it? For if he lays the foundation and is not able to finish it, everyone who sees it will ridicule him, saying, "This fellow began to build and was not able to finish." Luke 14:28-30 (NIV)

So how do you wrap up a book like this and put a bow on top? It is difficult to be sure, but I honestly prayed and asked the Holy Spirit to give me something significant and memorable to end with. This is the passage that my mind was drawn to.

No long lists will be unveiled in this chapter. No clever formulas will be revealed to finding true love. And I will not bore you with more statistics or stories. I just want to simply end with the words of Jesus, applying those words to the world of relationships and love.

Jesus understood the day he lived in. He did not withdraw from culture or boycott the world around him. He brought light into a dark place and he understood people, and he understood what they would understand. So he spoke like one of them, about things they knew and were familiar with.

When Jesus spoke these words, large crowds were following him everywhere He went, perhaps hoping for a free meal or a good show, or the healing of a sick child or a family member. But somehow, Jesus could look into every single one of their hearts and know the motive lying there. He knew why each of them was there, as a matter of fact one of the gospels even says that many people believed on Jesus, but He would not entrust Himself to them for he knew what was in their hearts. Jesus had X-ray vision and so it was in the context of a large crowd that he used an analogy of a man building a tower to convey a message to the people.

The question was about how much it would cost for one to be a follower of Christ. He did not play around. He cut to the quick. He told them that to follow Jesus meant to abandon worldly attachments. He warned them that there was a high price to be paid and then he used an illustration that was easily understood by common folk, religious zealots, and wealthy patrons.

He told them that they needed to first consider the cost of something as long term and demanding as being His disciple, just like a man should sit down and with careful planning and preparation consider how much it will cost to build a tower before he builds it. Was this a grain tower? A castle? A jab at the tower of Babel? I don't think it matters what kind of tower it was, and the text gives us little in the way of hints. The point is not the tower, but the preparation (or lack thereof) that should go into a major building project.

In that day, unfinished buildings were common, and little has changed. Money can run out before you know it. Bad weather, bad economy, or a bad stock market can lay waste to major building endeavors. This crowd had probably seen half-finished towers crumble to the ground. Who knows? Maybe Jesus was standing under one such tower or pointing at one in the distance as he issued this warning.

I think it would be appropriate at this juncture to apply this lesson from our Lord to our lives and relationships. If this one simple admonition is followed, then I truly believe all the heartbreak and drama would stop.

Consider the cost.
Can you finish the job?
Can you seal the deal?
Can you finish the relationship once you start it?
Can you carry this thing all the way to the end?

Our attitude must change from an apathetic one to a serious one about relationships and this question must be asked before taking someone's heart into your hands or before placing your heart in the hands of another; can I build this relationship to completion, or will I quit in the middle of it and be ridiculed for my inability to finish well?

Many of us have never thought about that, and it is the last question we would ever consider because we don't go into a relationship expecting it to last. We expect them to fail! And that may be the saddest, most lamentable thing I have said in this book. If you expect your relationships to fail, then they will. Why bother? This is the sorry attitude that seems to represent the average dating relationship.

But Jesus said that it was wrong to approach things this way. He advocated a thoughtful approach to life. In this case it was discipleship. In your case it may be relationships, which by the way fall squarely in the discipleship department if you are a believer.

People are not toys or pets. If things don't work out, you will not walk away in most cases unfazed. The heart is tender, and it has a memory. People get hurt really bad when things don't work out. So it is better to think long and hard and ask whether you have the character and integrity to stick it out.

This brings us to the center of the issue. There is no way in this world that we can, by trying harder or buckling down tighter, make things work. We are unable to achieve success by our own efforts. We must totally and fully rely on God to provide us with what He requires.

My God will meet all your needs according to his glorious riches in Christ Jesus. Philippians 4:19 (NIV)

Not only will God meet your needs for food and water and shelter, but He will provide your emotional needs, too. He gives us friends and parents and eventually He gives us a mate and children of our own. Why fret? Do you believe God is true? If so, then quit asking why you are not married yet! It is not time. You are not ready. When you are ready, God will provide your need. And when you prepare for marriage and enter into the covenant, God will provide you with the grace to finish the job. You will not have to muster it on your own.

And how does God provide us with all these things we need along life's journey? He does it through Jesus Christ, His own Son. It is through the death and resurrection of Jesus that we have all our needs met. Not just for life and forgiveness and heaven and joy, but also for relationships and the ability to finish them well.

This causes a problem for those who love the weekend romances or the one-night stands. It also makes it sticky for people who throw in the towel and get divorced for little or no reason. We really are left without an excuse here. What we toss out the door in the name of convenience or a desire for happiness God calls sin. You can make it work because God will give you the grace to finish it, if it was a relationship he wanted you to pursue in the first place.

Even our most crafty reasons and explanations don't hold water because we have been warned not to walk too easily into something so important. We are told to stop and assess our ability to finish what we start. We are told that in life it is better not to start plowing than to start and then stop. We are warned to count the cost and if we can't handle it, not to start it. Read this again...

When you make a vow to God, do no delay in fulfilling it. He has no pleasure in fools; fulfill your vow. It is better not to vow than to make a vow and not fulfill it. Ecclesiastes 5:4-5 (NIV)

Some of you are single and happy. Good for you. You are less likely to carry around regret and pain for the rest of you life. Some of you are in a Godly and healthy relationship that honors the Lord. Good for you. Stay pure and holy and honor God.

Others of you need to make a vow to God to stay single-minded and focused on God alone for a year. No dating or flirting or hooking up or any of that for twelve months, NO exceptions.

And still some of you are in a relationship right now that is wrong. It may be sexual sin or insecurity or any of the other wrong reasons to date someone. I am telling you for your own good to end it now. The sooner, the better. Don't postpone the inevitable. You will hurt more the longer you wait, and if you have considered the work it will take, and you are not willing to invest that kind of time and energy, I believe Jesus was clear. Don't even start until you can finish the job.

A few years ago at a small Christian college, I was preaching for four days in a row. The first night after my message on love and relationships, I issued a challenge to the students to pray and consider if they might be willing to make a one-year vow to God to stay single and single-minded, not dating at all for twelve months so they could develop intimacy with Christ. There was no manipulation and they had three full days to think about it. The campus lit up in a fire of controversy. It was all the students talked about that week and many of them were upset that a preacher would do such a thing. Others loved the idea. Some called it legalistic and others applauded it.

On the last night of the student revival, about thirty students made the commitment. I had no idea how many would keep it. I never do.

I came back a year later and found out that the whole thing had continued to grow in controversy and scandal after the revival was over. Some openly criticized it while others defended it (Remember the red flag of drama?). So when I arrived everyone was talking about it and wondering if I would address it. I did briefly on the first night, and a young lady stood up and said, "The reason why so many people got so bent out of shape over the one-year vow was that our standard for relationships on this campus is so low. Why were so many people offended that thirty of us made the vow? Is it because we embarrassed them and the way they do it? Keep raising the bar, Clayton, and don't ever listen to the critics."

I go back to that college every year, and since that night in 1999 I have met numerous students who made that decision and are now happily married. They all tell me it was the best thing they ever did. Why? They set aside time for Christ. They stepped back from the drama and madness of the dating roller coaster. They considered what a serious thing love really is, and when they started building a foundation, they were ready to go all the way, for life, and finish the job by God's grace.

You have taken the time to read this book. You have heard the verses and the explanations. You have reasoned through the logic. You have read sound, Biblical advice and directives in these very pages. Even if this is the only book you have ever read on love and relationships, you have read this one. Now, you are without excuse.

Marriage takes time, energy, patience, and effort. Even with all of these things, you are hopelessly doomed if you are not resting in the grace of God to make you the kind of person you must be to stay married for life. If you are not ready for that investment, whether you are too young, too immature, too indecisive, too spoiled, too selfish, too hurt, too scared, too bitter, too dramatic, too moody, or too vain, then don't even think about it! Wait until you are spiritually ready. When you have become the right person and God provides you with the right person, and you will have a lifelong relationship without regret.

Re-order Form for <u>Love, Dating, and Other Insanities</u>

If you would like to order another copy or multiple copies of this book, please fill out this form and mail it with your payment to **King & Furtick: P.O. Box 1448, Boiling Springs NC 28017.** Re-order books **cost $15** which includes shipping and handling.

Re-Order Form For Love, Dating, & Other Insanities

Name: _____

Shipping Address: _____

_____

Phone Number: _____

Number of Books Ordered: _____

Amount Enclosed: _____

Re-Order Form For Love, Dating, & Other Insanities

Name: _____

Shipping Address: _____

_____

Phone Number: _____

Number of Books Ordered: _____

Amount Enclosed: _____

Re-Order Form For Love, Dating, & Other Insanities

Name: _____

Shipping Address: _____

_____

Phone Number: _____

Number of Books Ordered: _____

Amount Enclosed: _____

More great books from Clayton King

Journals of A Madman
A collection of 30 true stories from around the world, these are the strangest, craziest, and most unbelievable things that ever happened to Clayton. One chapter will have you doubled over with laughter and the next will have you in tears. Some of the stories include:
*When Clayton was made the king of a village in the Himalayas
*The time God raised a baby from the dead in India
*Clayton is mistaken for Garth Brooks and gives his autograph to fans
*Clayton and friends get chased by the KGB in Moscow, Russia
*A national television appearance dressed in a kilt
*Catching malaria in Kenya, Africa
*Clayton meets the next Dalai Llama in the Himalayas
*Clayton gets kicked out of a Motley Crue concert
*Clayton meets the lead singer of the Red Hot Chili Peppers in India
*Picking up a death row hitch hiker in Louisiana
*Over 100 pictures to prove it!

The Beauty and The Mystery
This daily devotional was written by Charie and Clayton King as a supplement for daily time in the scripture. It is 50 chapters long and deals with issues of faith and life honestly and openly from personal experiences and insights gained in ministry, marriage, and mission travels. It is not a shallow devotional full of easy answers. We deal with anger, forgiveness, purity, failure, surrender, sacrifice, materialism, prayer, community, regret, temptation, and authenticity.

To order, send a check for $15 made payable to Clayton King to:
Clayton King
Journals of a Madman or **The Beauty & the Mystery**
PO Box 1448
Boiling Springs, NC 28017
claytonkinglive@aol.com
order online at www.divinecommunications.com

The History of Crossroads Worldwide

In 1987, God saved Clayton King as a 14 year old 8th grader. That night, he felt called to preach, though it had never been his desire to go into the ministry. Almost immediately, God began giving him opportunities to preach in the Carolinas and Georgia to churches, youth groups, and prisons.

In 1991, he entered college and continued to travel during his 4 years at Gardner-Webb University, preaching extensively in the US and overseas in Russia, Romania, Hungary, Jamaica, Africa, and India.

In the mid 1990s he began a summer camp called "Crossroads." That same year, the ministry became a non-profit organization. The summer camps continued, and a few years later Crossroads began offering Winter Conferences as well. About that same time, a missions program was started called Crossroads Worldwide, focusing largely on the Asian sub-continent. In 2004, Crossroads Ministries changed its name to Crossroads Worldwide.

In it's 8th year, Crossroads began adding other speakers to its roster; young men who traveled preaching and teaching at colleges, youth camps, conferences, retreats, churches, rallies, crusades, and revivals. Now there are 7 men who speak, preach, or teach for Crossroads Worldwide. Some of the speakers also do motivational speaking for public school assemblies which are not religious in nature, but focus on issues like peer pressure, alcohol abuse, drugs, violence, and staying in school.

Crossroads Worldwide has a vision of purchasing land in Western North Carolina and building a minsitry facility that can be used for conferences and retreats, as well as a place for pastors and missionaries to come on sabbatical or just for reflection and restoration. We also desire to preach the gospel to the whole world, disciple all believers, and assist the local church in any and all ways possible in seeing God's Kingdom come.

Crossroads Summer Camps

Crossroads Summer Camps began in 1996 and now host 2,500 campers and staff each summer from across the country. The camp is open to all denominations and focuses on discipleship, Christian worldview, and evangelism. Classes are offered daily on topics like prayer, witnessing, the gospel and other religions, the importance of church, and Godly relationships. There are two services daily with great worship and biblical preaching and teaching. Activities like rock climbing, paintball, rapelling, tubing, swimming, basketball, ultimate frisbee, a talent show, and soccer are offered daily.

Middle school and high school students and their adult leaders are offered seminars based on their age, maturity level, and specific needs and interests. Meals and lodging are covered in the camp cost as well as all other activities and seminars. Over 50 college students make up our summer staff. For info or a free DVD contact us today at 704-434-2920 or visit www.crossroadsworldwide.com

Crossroads Worldwide Winter Conferences

Winter Conferences began in 1998 and now host over 1,000 students each year. The conferences are held in Gatlinburg, TN during the Martin Luther King, Jr. holiday weekend in January. Each service offers great preaching and worship, and workshops are offered with a strong emphasis on community, authenticity, and apologetics. There is a conference for middle and high school students and a seperate, simultaneous conference for college students.

Speakers and musicians have included David Nasser, Vodie Baucham, Charlie Hall, Derek Webb, Brent Gambrell, Adrian Despres, Carl Cartee, and all the Crossroads Worldwide speakers. For more info or a free DVD, contact us today.

Crossroads Worldwide Speakers and Teachers

Crossroads Worldwide has a variety of men that can speak in a multitude of settings to various audiences. These men have experience, training, and accountability. Most of all, they have a call on their lives to share Christ with this world. If you are looking for a speaker, please contact us if we can assist you in any of your events.

Clayton King - Clayton began preaching at the age of 14 and has travelled in 45 states and 22 countries, speaking to over 2 million people. He addresses public school assemblies, college campuses, youth conferences and camps, and teaches on a variety of subjects ranging from missions to music to marraige. Above all, he is an evangelist who is passionate about the gospel. Adopted at 3 weeks old and raised on a farm, Clayton was taught to value authenticity. This comes through as he speaks with candor and humor.

Steven Furtick - A student of dividing truth for interpretation, Steven is a man on a mission! He can speak on just about anything but specializes in teaching on dating and relationships as well as evangelism. Steven will convincingly deliver truth to your group in a way that he has been truly gifted to do. Whether your group is large or more intimate, Steven can tailor a message for your group and even provide praise and worship for your event.

Derwin Gray - From the fields of the NFL to your group, Derwin Gray is a natural when is comes to communicating the truths of the gospel. He specializes in apologetics and shares his passion for truth with excitement and intelligence. Whether he is teaching you how to explain and defend your faith or showing seekers the way to Christ, he is as real as it gets. Whether it is a group of athletes before the big game or a group of teens who want a greater understanding of the gospel, Derwin is the communicator for you.

Matt Orth - Matt specializes in discipleship and verse-by-verse teaching. With a passion for truth and equal passion for seeing your group grow in deeper relationship with Christ and deeper community with each other, Matt can craft a weekend of training for your adult leaders or a discipleship weekend for your students. Either way, you and your group will come away with a greater understanding of the Word and a greater love for the Body of Christ.

Scott Ryan - Scott has been speaking since he was 17 years old to churches, youth groups, camps and retreats. He has spoken in many states on the East Coast as well as 3 different countries. He is a gifted communicator of the Gospel. His delivery is energetic, fun, and intelligent. Scott specializes in speaking to youth and college-aged students. His goal is accurate Biblical interpretation within the context in which the scripture was written and practical application to the lives of young and old alike.

Brian Burgess - As a full-time youth pastor, Brian has over 13 years of experience in ministry. He has spoken to youth and adults all over the United States. He has a zeal for life and enjoys physical fitness, riding motorcycles and spending time with his wife, Angie. Brian is the founder of "Toolin in Town" a ministry that reaches out the the often rough and tough world of Bikers. He has a Masters of Divinity and loves teaching students, singles, and young adults how to put their faith in Christ to work in every day situations.

Brad Borders - As a former full-time youth minister and current Army Chaplain, Brad has had great experience in all facets of ministry. He is a graduate of Southern Evangelical Seminary and has studied under some of the greatest professors in the United States, including Norman Geisler. He connects with crowds of all ages and thrives in any ministry setting.

For scheduling information:
Crossroads Worldwide Office
704-434-2920
crbooking@aol.com
www.crossroadsworldwide.com

Preaching Sermons available in DVD and CD

Clayton's Sermons are listed below and can be ordered online at divinecommunications.com:

"Take a Chance For God" - Story of a 1999 mission trip to the Himalayas where Clayton was made king of a village, the team was bombed by Muslims, and God raised a baby from the dead (Live @ Ridgecrest).

"The 4 C's of a Lasting Marriage" - Four Biblical and practical steps to being prepared for marriage or for making your marriage last a lifetime: Christ, Communication, Commitment, & Courtesy. (Live @ Cumberland College).

"True Belief" - A look at what belief really is instead of what our culture has made it to be. Do you have Inherited, Intellectual, or Intimate belief? A powerful evangelistic message for groups or individuals, young or old.

"Close To The Kingdom "- Message on how God uses unlikely people & how those we think are the farthest away are actually closer to Christ than we think. Great for those who are hurt or critical of faith. (Live @ Jars of Clay show)

"Love: More Than A Feeling" - Love has lost it's meaning these days, so what does it really mean to be in love? It means sacrifice & commitment, not just the dating fuzzies. (Live in Nashville, TN with 5,000 students).

"David: The Fall of a Great Man" - How one of the greatest men in the Bible failed God by being in the wrong place, having the wrong desires, actions, and reactions. The story of David and Bethshaeba (Live @ Mt. Lebanon, TX).

"The Gospel According To Jesus" - What did Jesus say about salvation compared to what we say today? A look at our cultural gospels, like the "Sweet Tea" and the "Hollywood" gospels compared to the bible.

"The 4 Hearts" - The parable of the farmer and the seed and how the soil represents our hearts before God: Hard, Shallow, Crowded, and Open. A great evangelistic message for seekers and skeptics. (Live @ Mt. Lebanon, TX).

"The Call To Ministry" - A practical message on what it means to be called into the ministry & where to get started, looking at numerous biblical examples of people God called & used. (Live @ Crossroads Ministry Summit).

"Lifelong Discipleship" - John the Baptist sets a great example of what a real disciple is as he always pointed people away from him and toward Jesus. Good for Christians who want to go the next level. (Live @ Crossroads Camps).

"Unity In The Kingdom" - A look at how the church worldwide is a Body and should work together for missions and evangelism, regardless of color or country. (Live @ YouthQuake in Jacksonville, FL to 3,000 students).

"Take Up Your Cross" – Jesus said to follow Him, deny ourselves and take up our cross. This phrase was like a curse to the Jews in light of a rebellion and hundreds of crucifixions and it must cost us something! (Live @ Dallas, TX)

"A Prostitute Meets a Prophet" - The story of Jesus and the woman at the well shows us how to treat others with mercy and kindness in order to show them God's love effectively. A great message on sharing your faith

Steven's Sermons are listed below and can be ordered online at stevenfurtick.com:

"Live Purity Series" - Messages from both Steven and Holly as they share their own stories and insights from their marriage about purity and holiness.

"Something More" - A sermon about the sufficiency of Christ in the daily walk of all believers.

"Building Your Life on Christ" - Taken from the very words of Christ, a message about building your life on the firm foundation of Christ instead of the shifting sands of anything else.

"Long Term Purity" - A great message about God's ultimate goal for us in relationships; marriage!

"How to Make Your Life Count for Nothing" - From the words of Paul, a message on total surrender to Christ, living for Him alone and not for your own agendas, name, recognition, or glory.

Adam's Housecat

Founded by Clayton King, Adam's Housecat began in 1997 after Clayton's first band, Monogamous Fish, disbanded. The band still plays today, leading worship at high school and college events across the country. Here are the records they have available.

Tag, You're It - $15
An album of all original rock and roll! If you like Third Day, Train, or Vertical Horizon, you will love this record. Full of hidden tracks and two versions of "The 'Rasslin' Song" made famous by Johnboy and Billy.

.Patience and Affliction - $15
Our first worship record. Some songs include "I Could Sing of Your Love Forever", "God's Gonna Rock This Place", "More Love, More Power", "Shout To The Lord", "Beautiful, Scandalous Night", and several old hymns.

The Least of These (Guest vocals by Mac Powell of Third Day) - $15
Recorded by former engineer for The Black Crowes, this worship album includes "Open The Eyes of My Heart", "In The Secret", "Agnus Dei", "There's a Stirring", "Amazing Love", "Better Is One Day", "The Old Rugged Cross", and many more.

Live at Crossroads Volumes I & II - $15
These records really are live, with no studio overdubs or tricks. As good as anything Passion has ever done, and truly live at Crossroads Youth Camps! Includes "God Of Wonders", I'm Trading My Sorrows", "We Are Hungry", "Freedom Song", "We Fall Down", "Give Us Clean Hands", and much, much more!

Monogamous Fish - "Life" - $25 (only 19 copies left)
Clayton's first band which started as a joke in 1995, but ended up actually happening! They toured twice, opened for Third Day, Rebecca St. James, and Smalltown Poets. For fans of Jars of Clay, early R.E.M, Toad The Wet Sprocket, and Stryper (just kidding about Stryper). A seriously great acoustic rock record with a killer sermon at the end.

To Order: Send check or money order made to Clayton King to:
**Clayton King - Adam's Housecat
(Name of Album You Want)
PO Box 1448
Boiling Springs, NC 28017
Order online at www.divinecommunications.com**

Great Ministries We Endorse

Emmanuel Ministries- Hopegivers International
www.hopegivers.com

The Voice of The Martyrs
www.vom.com
www.persecution.com

Clayton's Book List

For several years, people have asked me what books I would recommend for them to read in their walk with Christ, so I decided to compile a list of the books I have read that have impacted me the most. I do not agree with all points made in these books, nor do I equate them with the bible. However, these are the books God has used in my life in the most significant ways.

Mere Christianity - C.S. Lewis
The Normal Christian Life - Watchman Nee
The Cost of Discipleship - Dietrich Bonhoefffer
Here is There and He Is Not Silent - Francis Schaeffer
Basic Christianity - John R.W. Stott
The Release Of The Spirit - Watchman Nee
Let The Nations Be Glad - John Piper
My Utmost For His Highest - Oswald Chambers
The Great Divorce - C.S. Lewis
The Lord of The Rings - J.R.R. Tolkien
Transforming Mission - David Bosch
Just As I Am - Billy Graham
Tortured For Christ - Richard Wurmbrand
The Pursuit Of God - A.W. Tozer
God's Smuggler - Brother Andrew
Celebration Of Discipline - Richard Foster
The Call Of The Wild - Jack London
Coach - Keith Dunnavant
Jesus Among Other Gods - Ravi Zacharias